D1329086

FOUR BROTHERS IN ARMS

IAN McGILL

Published by

MELROSE BOOKS

An Imprint of Melrose Press Limited
St Thomas Place, Ely
Cambridgeshire
CB7 4GG, UK
www.melrosebooks.com

FIRST EDITION

Cover designed by Jeremy Kay

ISBN 978-1-907732-42-3

Printed and bound in Great Britain by:

Mimeo Ltd, Huntingdon, Cambridgeshire

FSC
www.fsc.org
MIX
Paper from
responsible sources
FSC® C019549

CONTENTS

"Four Brothers in Arms is a remarkable story of an indomitable military family whose sacrifice and service in India before, during and after World War 2 is so typical of many British families who served the British Indian Empire. Their letters also give a simple but moving account of the realities of war and of the people who daily faced danger, disease and hardship. I commend this book to a younger generation. It will help them understand better the extraordinary qualities of a previous generation of men and women who shaped our world today." General Sir Michael Rose, former Commander of the UN Protection Force in Bosnia.

"A story of a remarkable family, steeped in service in India, told through letters that the brothers sent, received and were written about them. They draw aside the curtain on some of the most momentous periods in the C20th from life in India before WW2, the fighting in Italy and Burma, the occupation of The Channel Islands, the Partition of India and the end of British rule in Rhodesia. The letters are fascinating, as fresh as the day they were written, and full of forthright views about people and events; and from a generation that was supposed to be emotionally repressed, they are full of feeling and sentiment." General Sir Jack Deverell, Chairman of the National Army Museum and former Commander-in-Chief Allied Forces Northern Europe.

"I much enjoyed the book. It reads really well and provides a wealth of insights into the profession of arms. It is also the story of a family bound together in peace and war by love, loyalty and service - to each other and to the Crown." Lieutenant General Sir John Kiszely, National President of the Royal British Legion and former Director of the UK Defence Academy.

"What a remarkable story!" Lieutenant General Sir Andrew Ridgeway, former Lieutenant Governor of Jersey.

PREFACE AND ACKNOWLEDGEMENTS

The catalyst for trying to piece together something about my father's and his brothers' lives was some letters I found long after my father died. Reading them for the first time I felt a growing admiration for how they and my grandparents had coped with the turbulence they faced during and after the war years. There is, inevitably, much missing from this account because records were lost, but it provides a series of snapshots about the brothers, together with an insight into their endeavours during a crucial period in Britain's history. It also gives a glimpse of the turmoil faced by my grandparents in Jersey at the start of the war and during the German occupation, anxious for news of their four sons serving far away from home. The three eldest brothers, Malcolm, Dick (my father) and Jerry, joined the Army in the early 1930s. Between them they served on the North-West Frontier of India; in Burma, where Malcolm the eldest was killed in action near Imphal; the Middle East; Africa and Italy. The youngest brother, Nigel, joined the Royal Marines, serving in the Mediterranean and the Indian Ocean before being attached to the American Eighth Army in the Philippines. After the war, Dick was tied up for a time with the chaos resulting from the India/Pakistan partition before starting an exciting new life in Rhodesia on a farm with a young family. Jerry and Nigel continued with their military careers, both serving at the same time in the Malayan Emergency in the early 1950s and eventually retiring in their early fifties to tackle civilian jobs.

After his death, Malcolm's belongings were sent to my father, who was then serving in Headquarters 14th Indian Division in Burma and soon to rejoin his battalion in Italy. One photograph album and a few letters from him are all that now remain. His medals were sent to me by the MOD medal office more than sixty years after his death and are now with Nigel, the youngest and sole surviving brother. Christoph Kohler (a cousin) sent photographs of the Commonwealth War Grave near Rangoon, where Malcolm's name is listed. The rector of St Clement's Parish Church, Jersey, sent photographs of a memorial at St Clement's, where Malcolm's name is one of those inscribed on the memorial.

My father and mother, Frances (also known as Fluffy), left many of their belongings and personal effects in India when they moved to Rhodesia in late 1947. After my father's death in 1971 at the young age of fifty-nine, my mother moved to Salisbury, Rhodesia (later to become Harare, Zimbabwe). A few years later she then moved to England. More belongings were lost and there are no letters about my father's war service in Burma, Africa or Italy. Fortunately, there are some photographs of his life, and a full account of his battalion's actions in Italy is recorded in the 8th Gurkha Rifles' regimental history. My father valued his time as a soldier and, I feel sure, would have enjoyed sharing his experiences more; sadly, he died when I was only twenty-five and too young then to appreciate fully what he had lived through.

Jerry retained a number of letters written during the war to and from his parents that ended up in his possession when my grandmother Emily died. He also kept a couple of photograph albums, the few letters written to him by my father during India's partition and many letters from Rhodesia. There are no letters from him about his own war experiences, save for two that he wrote to my grandparents from the North-West Frontier in June 1940; nor are there any letters about his time in Malaya. Although I grew to know him well towards the end of his life, he very seldom spoke about his experiences on active operations.

Nigel (when aged ninety) generously spared me time to relate just a few of his experiences as a Royal Marine and he also recalled what he could about his three elder brothers. His wife Margaret kindly provided a copy of extracts of a letter to her from my grandmother, describing her time in Jersey under German occupation, and also allowed me to use her recollections of her war-time journey to England from South Africa in order to marry Nigel. They both also searched for photographs included in this account.

The British Library (India Office Records, Asia Pacific and Africa Collections) sent me everything they could find in their archives relating to Malcolm and my father. Their surviving files are not complete but the documents included photocopies of their Indian Army Records of Service, together with some course reports on them and a few of their Confidential Reports. I visited the National Archives at Kew to track down the recommendations, made during the war, for Dick's DSO and Jerry's OBE. The Ministry of Defence's Historical Disclosures Branch in the Army Personnel Centre released a copy of Jerry's record of service.

1

PARENTS – HARRY AND EMILY

Father – Lieutenant Colonel Harry McGill, born 1872 in Poona, India. Died July 1940 in Jersey.

My grandfather presided over a very close and united family while his four sons were growing up.

My grandfather Harry was commissioned into the Indian Army with the 90th Punjabis. He served in the Boxer Rebellion in China in 1900 and in Mesopotamia against the Turks during the First World War, but was invalided out of the Indian Army in 1919 at the age of forty-seven. He died in Jersey in 1940 within a month of the Germans occupying the island and three weeks before his sixty-eighth birthday.

Mother – Emily (née Thoms), born 1877 in Dundee, Scotland. Died in 1954 in England.

My grandmother was stranded in Jersey as a widow throughout the German occupation of the island.

After my grandfather died it must have been a difficult five years for my grandmother Emily, left on her own for the rest of the war. She was very worried about her four sons far from home. Nevertheless, the messages she managed to send to them via the Red Cross and Channel Island Refugee Committee were always optimistic and cheerful, despite her hardships during the occupation, especially towards the end. She lost many of her possessions when the Germans burnt her furniture and books in order to keep themselves warm, when no supplies could reach the island due to the Allied blockade after D-Day.

2

EARLY SNAPSHOTS FROM INDIA

Harry and Emily with (from left)
Dick, Nigel, Jerry, Malcolm

Malcolm

Harry outside the Officers'
Mess, 90th Punjabis

Emily

The brothers' adventures started at an early age when my grandmother with Malcolm aged four, Dick (my father) aged two and Jerry, a three-month-old baby, were travelling in 1915 by sea from Liverpool to India to join my grandfather. They were torpedoed off Ushant, near Brittany, by a German submarine and returned to shore in separate lifeboats, before completing the journey via France. The youngest brother, Nigel, was born the following year in India.

3

GROWING UP IN JERSEY

Malcolm

Dick

Jerry

Nigel

On returning to Great Britain from India the family had no fixed address for a couple of years, alternating between Dundee in Scotland and Farnham in Surrey until they finally moved to Jersey in 1921. My grandfather had lived there previously in the late nineteenth century when his father (John) returned from India.

My grandparents never owned a house and the family lived in four different rented houses after settling in Jersey, the fourth called Bryn Y Mor at Beaumont, their home at the start of the Second World War. The four boys all went to Victoria College, as had their father and uncle (Harry and John) some thirty-five years earlier, where they were all talented sportsmen. Dick, Jerry and Nigel all played in the school's cricket, hockey and athletics teams while Malcolm was in the boxing and shooting teams. Dick was captain of cricket and Jerry was head of school.

Jerry, Nigel, Malcolm, Dick

They all enjoyed swimming in the sea, sand yachting on the beaches and the friendly lifestyle on the island with a number of good friends. It was a very happy upbringing and the brothers were close friends. Malcolm, being the eldest, was held most accountable for any of his brothers' misdemeanours and was remarkably tolerant about 'carrying the can', perhaps more than he should have been expected to. My father, Dick, was a great favourite with the girls and Nigel remembers the phone ringing often and various female voices asking, 'Is Dicky there?' Jerry, ever considerate, even used to clean Nigel's bicycle for him. Nigel generally got away with more than his three elder brothers and Dick recalled him sometimes being called Benjy (after the biblical favourite son, Benjamin).

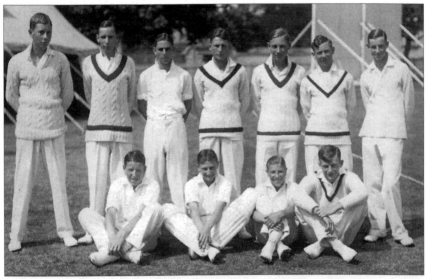

Victoria College 1st XI, 1930: Dick at centre of back row

Jersey v MCC, 1930: Dick, second from left in back row

4

LETTERS AND MESSAGES FROM AND TO PARENTS IN JERSEY DURING THE WAR

Letters to the three elder sons in India from my grandparents, shortly before the Germans occupied Jersey on 30 June 1940 (Nigel was in Portsmouth during this period)

Bryn Y Mor. Beaumont. Jersey.
8 June 1940

My dear little Dixy boy,

Thanks very much for your letter of 27th. Letters from Malcolm from Myitkyina dated 19th and Jerry also 19th arrived as well. Nigel's last letter did not contain any news. He says he has to work dreadfully hard & has to lecture on subjects of which he knows very little, so he has to swot these up at night. The weather is absolutely superb. Almost too hot to be pleasant. I can't enjoy life now like I used to, diabetes is a horrible disease. Great patches break out in various parts of the body, which irritate the skin. I'm in a hell of a funk I'll get a carbuncle on the back of my neck as there is a very irritating patch there. Dr Coutts has surpassed himself. I think I told you that some days ago I fell down unconscious after I had given myself an injection of Insulin, Coutts came and cured me at once by making me suck two lumps of sugar, for this visit because it was at night he has charged me 32/- 6d. Y.M. [your mother] called him in because she thought I was going to die. Insulin can have most peculiar effects. I had given myself an overdose.

Well; I'm glad you are having such a good time in Shillong. I won't say anything about the war; you can read all about it in the papers. Cope in the East Surreys, and Jack Nicholas are among those evacuated from Dunkirk. What an extremely clever gangster Hitler is. Every move is carefully thought of months ahead, and what makes me laugh is that it is all done on borrowed money. I am nearly blind so I hope you will pardon a lot of mistakes. I wish one of you boys were at home to drive the car, as we are nothing is done, I see no prospect of leaving this house, I can't walk and Y.M. is not much better, so between us we can't transact any business. I can type but I'm damned if I can write. I am nearly totally blind in the left eye and the right eye is gradually being affected. I have got to know a Mr Collins, a very wealthy man. He has bought Garden Court near the Bailiff's House. He seems a very kind hearted man, but Oh My Goodness; he is a terrible hypochondriac. He came here last night and brought me a new type needle for my syringe, much better than what I buy from Boots. He arrived at 9 and stopped till 1 a.m. and all the time he spoke about his stomach and his wife's stomach. Y.M. was desperate, we could not get rid of him, He has just come back from Australia, they had on board fifty refugee Jews from Germany of both sexes.

I met Major Hilton today; he was in the Liverpool Regt. He is now an Air Warden and was addressing some farmers here a few days ago about the danger of parachutists landing in Jersey. One farmer said, 'Where will they land? On the beach or on our fields?' Hilton said he could not say. Another farmer said, if they land on our fields they will steal all our potatoes. Now what are you to do with such fools. They can think of nothing but their damned potatoes. If the Germans could land about five hundred well-armed men here they would conquer the Island with the greatest ease. Of course there would be the difficulty of keeping them supplied with munitions etc. Young Joualt who joined the RAF has been awarded the DFC. Young Russell who was a St Luke's scholar at Victoria College with a Davis scholarship and joined the Staffordshire Regt, has been awarded the MC. You must remember him, his father was a soldier clerk in the Governor's Office. He entered the College in 1932 and left in 1939. Last night Y.M. came to my room and assured me she had heard bombs dropping, it turned out to be a false alarm. With Jersey so totally unprepared for invasion I am beginning to think we would be safer in England. The States [of Jersey] are living in a fools' paradise. Since you wrote your letter lots more has happened in Europe. I am going to send you the News Review, as the Editor shows Germany is nearly twice as big as she was in 1919 and most of it has been done without bloodshed, i.e. not actual war. The alliance with Soviet Russia has saved Hitler's bacon. If Russia had been hostile Hitler would never have embarked on this war with France and Britain.

Monday 10th. The news has just arrived that Italy has joined Hitler. I wonder what effect this will have in the USA. Even if they do join in, which I very much doubt, it will be at least a year before their help can be of much assistance.

What fools these youngsters are to get married in this state of the world, just try and realise what will happen if the Nazis win this war! Your career in India would be finished. Bang would go your prospect of any pension. Our Statesmen during the twenty years have been blind and criminally foolish, yet look at the way they treated Churchill because he warned them, it was

11

just the same before the last war. Lord Roberts warned the nation over and over again what was going to happen. He was looked on as a fool; in fact, Lloyd George said he was a danger to the peace of Europe and should have his pension stopped.

Tuesday 11th. An absolute glorious day. I met Mr Bell, the Times correspondent, he made me laugh, he is seventy-four and has just come out of the Limes after an operation for prostritis. He was anxious to do his bit, so volunteered to act as an Air Raid warden. He was given a rifle and posted to St Peters P.O. and Tel Exchange. He fairly sweated with funk, he had never fired a rifle in his life and had not the remotest idea how the damned thing worked. He loaded the rifle and put it in the corner and tried to sleep but it was impossible, he was terrified he might in his sleep waken up and press the trigger. Eventually he unloaded it with the help of the Postmaster who was an old militiaman. He tells me that even in Spain during the Civil War he never carried any arms. This was his protection. All the Spaniards, Italians and Germans were armed to the teeth.

I must close now, Y.M. is adding a sheet. I have sent Mal [Malcolm] and J [Jerry] some papers but I know you must have a very good club at Shillong, so I have not sent you any. If you want News Review, Illustrated Post, or War please let me know.
Ever your loving DADDY

Bryn Y Mor, Beaumont, Jersey, Ch Is,
21 June 1940

My dearest Malcolm & Jerry,

Still no letters from you but we wonder at nothing nowadays. Your letters won't come by airmail any longer so will go round by sea to the Cape and then to England. My letters to you will take just as long, but I will try and send you a joint letter each week, dear sons. We are living in such critical and swiftly moving days that nothing is certain. Jersey is now an open city & island, so we may have the Germans landing any day. All defences on the island have been removed & what exciting days we have just come through. Some days past two regiments, one from France & one from England, arrived here most unexpectedly & the noise all night long of large military lorries rushing past the houses kept us all awake. Guns were erected all over the island's coastline & we tumbled over troops. Just opposite our house there were two guns sited & crowds of soldiers were hanging around. I spoke to them each time I passed & several times I gave them a jolly good snack & they were so pleased & grateful. One sergeant was a particularly nice man, spoke well, was nice-looking & he told me he had done 4 years' service in India, been to Quetta & Razmak. He liked India very much, he said; he had been in the reserves for some years & was a bus driver in London till war began. He was charmed with Jersey & said how nice & hospitable we all were. Then yesterday they all suddenly got orders to embark for England as Jersey had been declared an open port. All the lorries rushed past again full of men and this evening, Mrs Douglas, Daddy and I spent three hours watching eight boats leave the harbour. They all met a convoy just beside the

*point. Thousands of people have left the island yester-
day & today & more leave tomorrow. Panic spread over
Jersey like wildfire and I have never seen such a sight.
The boats were crammed full, people herded like cattle, no room even to sit down. I knew there was no use
thinking of taking Daddy over like this, he would just
have died on the way. In the meantime we are making
enquiries and may leave for England later on when a
mail boat sails. If not then we will just have to spend
the remainder of the war here and pray all may be well.
Mrs Douglas has decided to do the same as us and in
the meantime we are going to live in her flat & share
expenses. It will be more cheerful for all concerned. The
Governor of course had to go as there are no defences
here now. If you don't get letters from us regularly don't
worry too much, it may be that no letters will be allowed
to leave Jersey, if the Germans should come.*

*England is impossible at present, full of hundreds of
refugees sleeping on the pavements, poor souls. Thousands from France are pouring in daily. I can hardly believe a year ago we were all so happily together at home
here, having a lovely summer and now all is changed to
sadness & desolation. Do you know hundreds of people
have left the island with only 15 lb of luggage; their
houses are left with all their belongings & furniture &
the streets and harbour are filled with hundreds of pri-
vate motor cars. It would be funny were it not so tragic.
All money has been sent from the banks to England and
it is terribly difficult to cash a cheque. I am going in
with Mrs Douglas tomorrow morning to try and cash a
cheque for £25, that is the most they will cash, and £25
does not go far for two people travelling. If we do go to
England, I'll try and send you a cable, Malcolm, telling
you where we are and will you please pass the information on to Jerry & Dick dear, as I can't send more than*

one cable. Of course it may be impossible to cable and I'll also write a letter. If possible I'll try & get rooms in Devonshire or Wales, but every place is crowded out.

I hope you had a nice time in Shillong, Malcolm dear, and that Dick was very well & cheery. Did you & Jerry manage to meet anywhere? Jack Nicholas called on us one evening last week; he was home on six days' leave from Dunkirk. He was looking well and never mentioned the fact that both his arms were wounded by shrapnel & one arm fractured. Jack never makes a fuss about himself. The weather is lovely but rather colder lately, a strong NE wind which is pleasant for any who have to work hard. A lot of the tiny tots from the crèche have been evacuated to Beaumont. They will enjoy the sands & the sea, I expect. Daddy has been out three times today and looks all the better for it. He is inclined to sit & think about himself too much and then gets depressed. People tell me his letters are most depressing but Daddy has always been inclined to write in a depressing way. He used to make me feel quite anxious and worried about him when we were apart in the last war when I was up in the hills with you children. But when I met him again he was in the best of health. I know he is not strong & never will be very strong again, but the mind plays a large part in one's health. He can't do much & I do take great care of him & watch his health carefully.

Must say goodbye now, my dearest ones. God guard you all.

Much love, Mother

Brn Y Mor, Beaumont, Jersey, Ch Is,
Monday 24 June 1940

My Darling Dick & Malcolm & Jerry,

Just a hurried letter to tell you Daddy & I are all right & that you must not worry about us too much. Crowds of English people are remaining here rather than go to England. Poor old England; she has enough on her hands without a lot of elderly & rather useless people. So cheer up & remember Daddy & I are going to live with Mrs Douglas at Netherby Court Flats, Beaumont. We can share expenses, which is a nice thing to do at present, also I can help her & she can help me and Daddy. We'll be well cared for & comfortable. Crowds of other people we know are remaining on Jersey. I considered all things very carefully before deciding, and consulted the Hulton's & health officer & others, & their advice was 'remain here'.

Jersey is now an undefended zone; all the troops that were here are now gone to England. I miss them very much, some of them were quartered just opposite our house & I used to give them snacks and meals that they much enjoyed & were most grateful for. Even the Jersey Militia under Col Hatcher have gone. We are under civil rule now the Governor has gone, & sorry he was to go & so was his wife. We have lived through days of panic & anxiety, but I am certain that God will be with England and all her men & women & we shall live to see dear old England or rather Great Britain a free & victorious country. Don't worry about me, everyone says how well & calm I am, I am naturally very worried and anxious about all my sons, & feel we may not be even able to receive & send letters to each other; but there are many others in the same position & you will, each one of you, be constantly in my thoughts & prayers & I hope you will do the same for Daddy & me. When I looked at our soldiers and sailors & all the French ones who were on leave here, I feel they act like a tonic; they are all so jolly & brave & cheery. We shall leave this house as it is, and Mrs Reilly will come in once a week and clean it, I will look in on passing to air it & open it up. Living with Mrs Douglas will be much nicer and easier for me and be better for Daddy.

Are you still in Shillong, Dick dear? We have had no letters from any of you for three weeks now, that is caused by the airmails being suspended. Go on writing to us by ordinary mail each week & I shall do the same to you. Send this letter on to Malcolm & Jerry, please Dick, as I cannot write any more today. Just written to Nigel and now have to go out & post them at the GPO. Daddy was able to go out for a long run in Mrs Douglas's car & have tea out in the Watsons' garden. I have the use of Mrs Duncan's nice hut at St Queens and all the people at Netherby Court have cars and we share & share alike with petrol & cars, which is very pleasant & friendly. Mrs Duncan went off in a great hurry to St Malo for safety and was bombed the first night she was there!

Must finish now & will write again soon & remember to pass letters on to each other. Much dear love & thoughts & may God have you all in his protection and guidance.

Your Mother

Bryn Y Mor, Beaumont, Jersey. 27/6/40.

My dear old Malcolm,

There is practically no news. No letters from India have arrived this week. Yesterday I posted the usual papers to you and Jerry. I don't send them to Dick because I realise there is a good club at Shillong where he can get them. Tomorrow we move into Mrs Douglas's flat. The address will be c/o Mrs Douglas, Netherby Court, Beaumont. We have chucked all idea of going to England, for several reasons. I am so weak that I doubt if I could stand the journey, we have no place to go to in England, several people who went there have returned and say we are much better off in Jersey, one lady told your mother she was in England only a week and was bombed three times. If we were both young and fit, we would go over at once, but the journey, followed by searching for accommodation, would just kill me. I MUST get my Insulin injection regularly three times a day or I will go blind and die; as it is I have entirely lost the sight of my left eye. I never realised before what a horrible disease diabetes is. If Dr Coutts had started treating me two years ago I would never have reached this state; as it is he allowed the disease to get a firm hold of me, and it is now well advanced and impossible to cure. All I can hope is that it won't get any worse. We are in a very awkward predicament; the banks refuse to cash any cheques, so we can't get any money. I have had to write to Cook and ask him to send me my pension by money order. Everyone here is in the same predicament. There have been some scathing letters in the papers about the way the Bailiff has bungled this crisis. Nothing has been done. I told you in my last letter the awful mess the States [States of Jersey] *made about the evacuation, thousands were allowed to go and given free passages, an absolute panic set in, some of the farmers turned their cattle loose, also their pigs and poultry, and cleared off. Thousands thought this was a fine chance of getting a free excursion to England, where they would at once get well-paid work in the munitions factories, or, failing that, they would draw the dole and be able to live without any work. I told you Jersey has been declared an open port; there no troops or defences of any sort. So I don't think there will be any bombing, though the Nazis may occupy the island and hold it to ransom. We are very concerned about Nigel because of course Pompey is sure to be a very likely objective for the German bombers. There has been no letter from him this week. I have no time to write to Dick and Jerry, will you please send this on to them. The weather is most peculiar, invariably damned cold bleak mornings followed by glorious afternoons. I managed to crawl as far as the village, by sitting down every hundred yards and resting. Y.M. is having a lot of extra work thrown on her by my illness. At Mrs Douglas's we will have a maid all day, not only for three or four hours, as is the case with Mrs Riley. Somehow I am not very happy about this move. I've never known two women to live together for long without having a row. However, if this occurs we can come back here. Do you know ALL the flats in Netherby Court are vacant; the occupants have gone to England. Ditto at St Breleads, and Vine Park. I think I told you Godfrey had bolted owing a lot of money, this is most inconvenient because we now have to send to town for everything. We are all wondering what Hitler's next move will be. He is no fool, every move is thought out very carefully before it is put into operation. Something which we least expect will suddenly be sprung on us. Well; no more news.*

I hope you are fit. We are looking forward to your first letter from Landi Kotal telling us about your meeting with Dick.

Ever your loving DADDY

Written the day before the German occupation

c/o Mrs Gordon Douglas
16 Netherby Court
Beaumont
Jersey, Ch Is
29 June 1940

My very dearest Malcolm & Jerry,

Still no letters from any of you which is sad, but we understand the reason. I hope you are now beginning to get letters from me every week. Since the airmails ceased I have posted a letter every week to you, one time I send it to you, Malcolm, another week to Jerry, & ask you to forward it. This is bound to be a rather disjointed letter as we have lived a hundred years in the last ten days. So much has happened to the whole of our lives and ways of living. Still I do not complain, it is awfully nice for me living here with Mrs Douglas and we have lots of friends in Netherby Court, so we are not lonely, which is a great blessing & comfort in these times. Daddy will soon settle down in his new home & he has a lovely large bedsitting room near to the large bathroom & lavatory & he has a lovely bed & writing table & armchair & central heating & hot & cold basin in his room. Large cupboard & chest of drawers, etc. so he has nothing to complain about.

I have a small bedroom but very comfortable & have my own hot & cold basin & bathroom just next door to my room. Daddy & I are of course paying our expenses & share of the rent, etc. Hundreds of Jersey people have left during the three days' evacuation & naturally a good many English as well. I hear about six thousand have returned, as they could not find accommodation in England. One gentleman returned to Jersey yesterday; he told me he was bombed three times in two days and could not find decent rooms anywhere, so is glad to be back here. Mrs Riley & her husband & sons left in the panic & hurry but came back in four days.

Had I been alone & [with] only myself to think of, I would have gone over by the Mail Co this week & gone to live with Auntie Grace & Uncle Bernard & Rachel & their children, but Daddy could never have done that long journey in his present weak condition. It would have finished him & I saw that at once, so decided to remain in Jersey & take care of him. Well, we must all do our best & help each other & trust & pray that dear old England & Scotland & Wales may win through & those devils be justly punished for all the misery they have caused. The cinemas each have 2 performances daily now; one at 2.15 & the next at 5 p.m. There is a curfew here each night now at 10 p.m. That does not worry me. I don't want to be out after 10. It is sad & hard for the young, but they are all so good & cheery & brave. Some shops are closed, all those belonging to Jews. The owners bolted at once, but all the large & principal shops are open & we have two mail boats a week. I am leaving all the furniture, etc., in the house [Bryn Y Mor]. I can't do anything else. All the furniture stores are full up & can't take any more. I can go and air the house & Mrs Riley comes in twice a week to clean the rooms. Lots of other people are doing the same & two families are sharing one house to avoid expense.

Daddy has come in from his walk & I must go & give him his tea. Don't allow his letters to depress & worry you all, because though far from strong, he is not nearly so bad as he thinks. He can see things at a great distance & reads quite a lot & eats well & sleeps well, & looks so much better. If only he could get stronger & be able to go out more, he would be much better. But after all, your old Daddy did not take much thought for his health during twenty years & more so he can't expect to be cured & feel fit in four months' treatment. Anyway, he is in good hands; Mrs Douglas is a thoroughly trained nurse & nursed her own husband for five years & she understands anyone like Daddy & is very nice & kind to him. Am going out for a run with Mrs Douglas in her car after tea so must say au revoir for the present. Will try & send a joint letter weekly to you, my dear sons, but if you don't hear regularly don't worry. Everything is bound to be upset. So long as you are well that is all I mind. God bless and guard each one of you & bring us together again in His good time. I think of you all the time and am lucky in having four such dear kind sons.
Goodbye & much fond love
Yours ever lovingly

Mother

Some messages via the Red Cross and the Channel Islands Refugee Committee

After the Germans occupied Jersey, the only means of getting messages to and from the island were by telegrams via the Organisation of the British Red Cross and Order of St John (limited to twenty-five words) and messages relayed through the Channel Islands Refugee Committee, 20 Upper Grosvenor Street, London W1.

Copies of some of the Red Cross messages sent to Emily and her replies are:

6/12/40 from Mrs Mildred Brewer [a friend] to Harry McGill: 'Letter from boys. India all well. Very anxious to hear from you. Please write me here.'
28/3/41 reply from Emily: 'Thanks for good news of boys. Sadly regret Harry died last July. I am well and with friend. Please communicate with Dick, Love to all.'

4/8/42 from Jerry: 'A F McGill asks us to inform you that your four sons are well and Dick is married. Your reply will be forwarded.'
9/12/42 (reply): 'Delighted receive message and learn my four sons well. I send love and greetings to all. Frances included. Am well and cheery. See friends often.'

11/12/42 from Dick: 'Am wondering if you have received my letters. Marvellous news you are now a grandmother to another Richard born in November. Lots of love.'
9/4/43 (reply): 'Dearest Ones, Warmest love, congratulations. Special kisses little Richard. Your letters received. Have answered all. Mrs Douglas sends best wishes. Weather lovely. Am well. Greetings.'

1/3/43 from Jerry: 'All my love and best wishes. We are all well and always think of you. Dick and Frances have presented you with a grandson.'
5/6/43 (reply): 'Thanks welcome letter. Visiting Mrs Douglas. Am very proud grandmother. Longing to see you all. Mrs Hulton enquires about you. I live in town. Dearest love.'

28/7/43 from Jerry: 'All well. Thankful hear good news you Uncle Alfred. Nigel in England. Think you grand. Admire courage. Looking forward surfing. God bless take care you.'
25/10/43 (reply): 'Delighted hear all well. Thinking of you always, also looking forward. Am well and cheery. God bless and guard you all. Dearest love and greetings.'

30/9/43 from Jerry: 'All going strong. Nigel gone home. Think of you always. Bless you for your courageous cheerfulness. Living for the day when we see you again.'

6/4/44 (reply): 'Glad all well. I living for day when we shall meet. God grant it soon. Delighted Nigel's engagement. Margaret nice name. Am cheery. Dearest love.'

Copies of two messages from the Channel Islands Refugee Committee (from Mrs Broome) to Jerry are also shown:

4 January 1944: 'Dear Colonel McGill, thank you for your letter. I have today sent off your message to your mother in Jersey and will let you know as soon as a reply comes through. We have very little interesting news of Jersey, apart from what comes through in the Red Cross messages. We have, however, had some fairly recent information about conditions in Guernsey. I have today written to your brother in South Devon sending him one of the leaflets which this committee issued, giving an account of these conditions. I hope he will find it interesting. I have also sent, under separate cover, one of these leaflets to you. We believe conditions are much the same on both islands and I hope you will get some idea of how those who remained behind are living. I hope it will not be too long before the islands are reoccupied and you are reunited with your family. The news now is very encouraging. With all good wishes. Yours sincerely, PM Broome.'

18 April 1944: 'Dear Col McGill. Thank you for your airmail lettercard of 1/4/44. The message to your mother has been sent. Replies are taking even longer now, I think. When it comes I will send it to you at once. We always hope that before so very long the need for messages will be over before long. Am sorry there is no further news to send on to you. We continue to do our best for the Refugees here, the Prisoners of War and those who were deported from the islands. Beyond clothing parcels, books and cigarettes there is nothing we can do for prisoners of war. We have now traced a good number of Channel Islanders who were in Station Prisoner of War Camps. All good wishes. Yours sincerely, PM Broome (Mrs)'

Extract from a letter from Grandmother Emily to Margaret (Nigel's wife) very soon after the Germans left Jersey when the war was finally over:

Now to tell you a little bit about life in Jersey during the Hun's occupation. So long as food could be brought here from France we did not starve but we were always hungry and I lost nearly two stone. Many people lost five stones in weight. My nice French doctor told me to go to bed with a good book and not to worry. I took his advice as much as possible and so have not lost nearly as much weight as lots of my friends. Our hardest and most terrible months were after France was invaded by the Allies. Starvation stared us in the face all last winter. We had nothing to eat except pig potatoes, swedes and a little bread, substitute tea made out of beetroot or leaves of such plants as the bramble, etc. No butter; no sugar; no jam or marmalade; no eggs and very often no milk. Hundreds of people died. Then the wonderful news came 'The Red Cross ship Riga is arriving in Jersey with lots of food'. Many people kept their wireless sets hidden under the ground, or in tin boxes in the ground. My friend Mrs Douglas had her wireless in her wardrobe with some dresses hanging over it. How she escaped being sent to prison I cannot imagine. Anyway she was able to tell me the news when we met, and dozens of other people as well. It really kept us alive.

Then electricity stopped. The Germans took the oil and had their own separate plant; then no gas or coal, but even that did not stop us hearing the news, hundreds of people on the Island made crystal sets and used part of their telephone as earphones. Anyway we were always able to listen in or hear the news from someone who did. We all ran a great risk, as the Gestapo were everywhere. Three times they came to my little house and questioned me. I could truthfully say I had no wire-

*less. The Germans took mine from me 4½ years ago,
and sent it to Germany. They took everything they could
from us – houses, furniture, cars, buses, lorries, cycles,
handcarts and food but one thing they could not take –
our firm belief in the British Army, Navy and Air Force
and in our wonderful Empire (and all the help – food –
sent to us).*

*The Huns sent a number of people in Jersey and
Guernsey to concentration camps in Germany. My name
was on the list and they were searching for me fourteen
days before they traced me here. I had left our home in
Beaumont, then spent some months with Mrs Douglas
and after that I came to this little place. When they arrived one morning to say I had to go to Germany and
to be ready to leave in twelve hours I nearly collapsed,
but managed to be polite to the Germans. The moment
they departed I put on my hat and coat and walked up to
the College House, headquarters of the Commandant. I
was interviewed by at least seven German officers, told
my story and stated there was no reason why I should
be sent to Germany. They replied: 'You are the widow
of an Army officer and you have four sons all on active service.' I looked at them all and replied, 'Yes, and
I am proud of them!!' That settled it. They smiled and
went away into another room. After an hour they came
back and took me to another room where the Commandant himself interviewed me. I again stated my case. He
said, 'Are you. British?' I said, 'Yes.' 'Are you English?'
I said, 'No.' 'What are you, then?' he asked. 'Scotch,' I
replied. They all shook hands again with me and said
'Madam, you can remain in Jersey.' I thanked them and
went out a free woman, thank God.*

*It was one of the saddest sights imaginable to see
those people leaving in boats. They were packed like
coolies, but as they left we could hear them singing*

songs, such as 'There'll always be an England.' I had tears pouring down my cheeks, and so had many others. I do hope you will be able to read this. We can't buy ink yet, so I have had to water mine. Funny little necessities such as shoelaces, buttons, elastic, toothbrushes, toothpaste, soap, hair fasteners and clips, hairnets – we can't get them here. I expect soon, however, they will arrive. I have been waiting eighteen months to have a pair of shoes resoled and heeled, and can't get them repaired. The soles of the shoes have big holes in them. My stockings are generally odd as we have not a pair fit to wear. I am luckier than many of my friends. I do have three pairs of fairly decent ones left from some I bought six years ago. I have let my hair grow past my waist, as I would not enter a hairdresser's shop while the Germans were here. Germans were everywhere. They crowded all the cinemas and showed German films. I have not been anywhere for five years, but they have never come to turn me out of <u>this</u> house. They were living in our home Bryn Y Mor at Beaumont. The flats at Beaumont were packed with them. They behaved quite well until they realised victory was ours, then they let themselves go and smashed up everything in the houses they occupied and used furniture for their fires. Hundreds of beautiful trees have been cut down as fuel by them. We had no fires, no gas, no electricity all last winter, and practically no food. We took our potatoes and swedes and carrots to bake houses. Every district had one. I was very fortunate and have had my meals – dinner and supper – at a boarding house. We were often nearly starved, but managed to laugh through it all.

I must come to an end and hope I have not wearied you too much. It is so wonderful to be able to write what one wishes after five years' silence – Thank God it is over.

5

MALCOLM

Major J M (Malcolm) McGill
Born 20 October 1910 in Dundee, Scotland. Killed in Action 26 June 1944 near Imphal

Commissioned from Sandhurst into the Indian Army in January 1931 and attached to 1st Battalion Norfolk Regiment until March 1932 before joining 2nd/9th Gurkha Rifles (GR). Attached to the Burma Military Police and Burma Frontier Force for four years from June 1936 and awarded a Special Mention by Commissioner of Police, Rangoon in October 1939 for his actions in 1938 at Yunnan Yang oil fields, the Rangoon riots, Tharrawaddy and Prome. Rejoined 9th GR in 1940, serving as a company commander with both 2nd/9th and 3rd/9th and as temporary Second in Command (2 i/c) of 3rd/9th GR in 1941. After six months at the Staff College, Quetta, in 1942 he served as a staff officer in Assam and Lahore before rejoining 3rd/9th GR in September 1943 as 2 i/c. Posted to 1st/7th GR as 2 i/c in January 1944, he was wounded in action (shot in the left lung) in March and rejoined the battalion in April. Acted as Commanding Officer (CO) for three weeks in May/June after the CO was wounded. After a further spell in hospital with dysentery he returned to active duty as the temporary 2 i/c of 2nd/5th GR. The day after joining his new battalion he was killed by a Japanese artillery shell.

Malcolm, while serving with the Burma
Frontier Force – middle row, fourth from left.

Malcolm back home on leave before the war

After four years with 2nd/9th Gurkha Rifles Malcolm opted for service with the Burma Military police and the Burma Frontier Force for the next four years, where his reports indicate that he was highly regarded, looking after his men particularly well. While with the Burma Frontier Force he was commended by the Commissioner of Police, Rangoon for duties in connection with civil disturbances in 1938.

A year after returning to the 9th Gurkha Rifles, Malcolm then attended the Staff College in Quetta, on the same course as Dick and passing out in the top half of the Order of Merit.

*Map from the Univesity of Texas
Online Collection
www.lib.utexas.edu/maps Courtesy of
the University of Texas Libraries, the
University of Texas at Austin.*

*Outline Map of Burma (in white).
Arrow points to location of Imphal,
across the border with India. The
scenes described in Malcolm's letters
took place around Imphal.*

**Letters from and about Malcolm in 1944, describing the intense
jungle fighting around Imphal and the very difficult conditions.**

*1st/7th Gurkha Rifles, SEAC [South East Asia Command],
13 May 44*

My dear Jerry,

*Many thanks for your letter of 20 Apr, which arrived a
week ago – not bad going. Letters are coming in quite
quickly these days now that the mail is flown in, although
mail from India still seems to take longer in reaching
me than letters from overseas. Along with yours I also
received a letter from Nigel, who now appears all set
for the matrimonial stakes. I wonder what his girlfriend
Margaret is like? So far I've been told very little about
her, although Nigel has quite excelled himself lately in*

matters of correspondence. I was so sorry to hear about Betty Sutton's husband being wounded. It's a long time since I saw her but I'll always remember her as a grand girl. Pity you & she didn't marry – she would have suited you. I've just had some more letters from Connie – she's a good sort to carry on writing to me, because I sometimes feel that our prospects of meeting each other again are rather remote. Canada sounds a marvellous country, & if any jobs are going there after the war I might chuck the army & try my luck there.

Since our last show life has been fairly quiet as far as the battalion is concerned. The Jap 18th Army Group set out early in March with the intention of destroying our forces in Chin Hills & Imphal area – but so far all he has received is a bloody nose & nothing to show for it, unless our withdrawal from Tiddim & the Chin Hills can be considered an asset. His attempt to capture Kohima has been foiled and he has had to give up his intention of advancing further west to Dinapur & cutting the Assam railway. His forces in this area and north of Imphal have been badly mauled, and two of his divisions have been partially destroyed. With only mountain tracks along which to supply his troops in this area & the monsoon close on us, he will have to withdraw east. To the south of Imphal his 31 & 33 Divisions are now trying to advance along the Tamu-Palel road & the Tiddim road. These are good MT roads & he has bought up tanks & medium guns. The RAF, Indian Air Force and USA Air Force, however, have undisputed freedom to bomb him as much as they like & he is not making much headway. To sum up he has lost at least 7,000 killed, inflicted by our ground troops alone, & quite a lot more from our arty & air action. Our losses have been very small in comparison. The Jap finding himself unable to make much progress along the roads has resorted to his usual flanking movements through the hills. By doing so his forces are dispersed in small packets in hills surrounding the Imphal plain, and our main job at present lies in driving them off. This we have done quite successfully. Last week the brigade was given the task of capturing a Jap position in a Naga village on top of a high hill. The day prior to the attack the RAF came over & bombed the Japs good & proper. I was doing a recce at the time & had a grandstand view across the valley of the whole proceedings. Vultee Vengeance dive bombers, five squadrons of them, came over in waves, circled above the Japs & then came down on them with all they had. The whole place seemed to go up in smoke & fire. We attacked at 0430 hours. The approach lay up three parallel spurs. It rained hard all the time & the night was inky black. The Japs heard nothing & our leading companies were in amongst them with grenade & bayonet before they knew what was happening. The previous day's bombing had flattened the village & killed quite a number & we killed nearly a hundred. The village was full of stiff Japs & smelt like a slaughterhouse. The remnants fled east along the ridge to be caught & wiped out by one of our commando companies. It was a well-planned & executed little operation, & yielded good results in the way of prisoners, equipment & documents. We returned to our billets in a Manipur village & tomorrow we leave on another mission which promises to be a tough & unpleasant business.

Among the fellows I've met recently have been Vic Whitehead, now commanding a battalion of the 8th, & Vickers, a contemporary of mine at Sandhurst who now commands a battalion of the 10th Gurkhas. COs are getting younger every month & I look like being left behind. However, they soon get the bowler hat if they boob, & I prefer to learn a bit more about fighting be-

fore I go up. GS, who got command of a battalion in the Arakan, lasted three weeks. He is now back in India. Hugh Conroy, whom you may remember, is also a CO now. The staff is being milked of officers who are being sent back to their regiments. I sometimes wish I had never gone to the staff, because I forgot a lot of stuff that I'm now having to learn again! I was interested to hear that Gertie Tuker had returned to India – I wonder what his new job is?

Well, old boy, enough for the present.

All the v best,

Malcolm

1st/7th Gurkha Rifles, 16 ABPO
[Advanced Base Post Office], 17 June 44

My dear Dick,

For the first time in nearly six weeks I find myself in a place where I can write some letters in reasonable comfort. In my last letter I gave you rather a long-winded account of the 1st/7th exploits in the road block affair at M.S.33 on the Tiddim road in the rear of the Jap's 33 Division. During that show we accounted for 267 Japs killed – bodies counted on the ground – & probably put paid to at least another 50 killed & 100 wounded, besides knocking out 4 tanks, destroying a number of lorries & capturing a large number of rifles, LMGs, swords & Jap flags. Subsequently we moved north with the remainder of the brigade, and after some very hard fighting, during which our role was reversed & we had to do the attacking, we finally worked our way around the Japs & joined up with the other brigades in our division. The monsoon had broken while these events were happening, & the conditions under which we had to advance & attack the Jap positions were just about as unpleasant as they could be. We were no longer in the hills but had to fight on the plain, this being mainly flooded paddy fields & quite devoid of any covered approaches. In the circumstances, therefore, it was not surprising that our casualties were fairly heavy – mostly among our platoon commanders & NCOs whose loss we could ill afford. After the show put up by all ranks, we all expected to be relieved & given a real good rest. Unfortunately this was not to be so. We established ourselves in a village not far from Bishenpore, which had been the scene of some fierce fighting the previous month. The place was littered with derelict tanks, both ours & the Japs', & we had a very unpleasant time burying the numerous corpses, which were lying around all over the place & smelling to high heaven. A few busy days were spent digging & wiring, & generally buttoning up the defences, the idea being to hold the Japs who were just south of us, while another brigade attacked them in the hills a few miles to the west. The Japs were reported to be concentrating & our patrols bumped into them every night. Finally on the night 6/7 June at midnight we were attacked in great force. A part of our perimeter was overrun & the situation looked fairly grim. It was pitch dark & pouring with rain, & the general discomfort was not improved by the yelling & screaming of the Japs, who were vainly trying to broaden the bridgehead that they had secured. I managed to collect a spare platoon & a British Officer named Jim Moloney led them in a counter attack that ultimately succeeded in driving out the Japs, but poor Moloney was killed. Next morning our perimeter was a shambles. The Japs had withdrawn to the hills, but had left a number of 'do or die' snipers, who made life most uncomfortable for all of us throughout the day & we only succeeded in liq-

uidating them after knocking down the bunkers & bunds behind which they were installed by using 2-pounder anti-tank guns & masses of grenades. After the whole show was over we counted seventy-three bodies, including a major, captain & two subalterns. A captured document subsequently revealed that a whole battalion had attacked us & the dead major was the commander. Of course the total strength of the battalion had been much reduced. Very few Jap battalions in this area are now at full strength & the majority have been reduced to a strength of less than 400. For this show we received a personal shabash from Punch Cowan & Scoones.

We then had two comparatively peaceful days, & were then moved south to relieve the Red Toggles in another village where conditions were even more unpleasant, Rain had been falling unceasingly for several days & the whole place was & still is a quagmire. The village, such as it is, is divided by a stream into two sections. We occupy the north section, while on the other side of the stream are the Japs. All the houses had been completely destroyed during a previous battle & there was hardly a square yard of dry ground. We built a lot of new bunkers as much above the level of the water as possible – but more rain swelled the stream running through the middle of the village & also the large lake to our east. On the night of the 11th the Japs attacked again with several tanks & at dawn succeeded by some extraordinary means in getting the tanks across the flooded nala & penetrated the forward positions. We counter attacked immediately with a couple of companies & sent forward some PIATs & 2-pounder anti-tank guns. The tanks had got into our position & were less than fifty yards from Battalion HQ. Fortunately the mud was too much for them & they fell an easy prey to the PIATs & anti-tank guns, no less than five being completely destroyed – all medium tanks. We hope to get them hauled out of the mud & sent back to India for exhibition because these happen to be the first medium tanks captured by us.

On the 12th, 13th, 14th, 15th the rain continued to fall in buckets & conditions became indescribable. Our bunkers were all completely flooded. I almost had to swim out of mine in the middle of the night & all my kit, fortunately very little, was completely destroyed or lost. To visit various parts of the perimeter meant wading up to one's waist in muddy water. All the graves which had been dug by the Red Toggles were uncovered by water & scores of corpses, in various stages of decomposition, floated into our area. All most unpleasant & unsanitary. The water used for drinking is heavily chlorinated but I shudder at the thought of drinking it. I prefer to have it boiled & served as tea, & then I know it is reasonably safe. Food, considering the circumstances under which it is cooked, is really not too bad. We are continually soaked & never have the chance of drying our clothes.

Well there's the full tale up to date. A few days ago Colonel McDowell turned up to take over command temporarily until Jim Robertson returns. I felt a bit peeved because I see no point in being 2 i/c unless one is considered fit to command in the CO's absence. But such things happen. One never knows where one is these days. Basil McDowell is really rather a good bloke & we get on very well.

I am now taking two days off & having a rest & clean up in our dump at Imphal. The thought of returning to the forward area depresses me quite a lot!

Hope young Richard is OK again & that life in Chindwara is not too bloody.

My love to Fluffy & Richard.

Yours aye Malcolm

PS. So wrapped up with myself I forgot all about the

marvellous news from Europe. Shouldn't be too long before Jersey is reoccupied by us – marvellous to think of it, what?

1st/7th Gurkha Rifles, South East Asia, 24 June 44

My dear old Jerry,

How are things with you? Your last letter was dated 13 May & I can't remember if I replied or not. I am now in hospital again – but not wounded this time. For nearly three weeks I have had the squitters – it became rather too much for me especially when our one & only latrine became a target for Jap snipers & mortars! So I had no other course but to go to bed for a few days & the only place for that was hospital! The doctors are now busy filling me up with special pills, which are acting like concrete & are bunging me up like concrete! Most of us are suffering from this embarrassing & distressing complaint in varying degrees of severity – brought on by the filthy water we have in these parts. The place we are in is lousy with corpses, mostly Jap, and simply crawling with maggots & other germs. It beats me why all of us aren't down with dysentery & typhus. Until I went to hospital I hadn't had a bath or change of clothes for a month, & more than once I found lice on my body – rather disgusting thing to write about, I know, but what can one do!

Had cryptic letter from Nigel the other day. He had everything teed up to marry Margaret on 24th. I find it strange to think of him being a married man – but I suppose people at home think it much stranger for a bloke my age to be a bachelor still! He is now a major & is doing a course at some CTC [Commando Training Cen-

tre] in Scotland. Rather mysteriously he said something about possible seeing Connie Lailey in the near future – I wonder what that means.

Isn't the news wonderful! You blokes in Italy have been marvellous in winkling the Bosche out of central Italy & Rome so quickly. I wish we could do the same with the Japs. The latter, once he is allowed to do so, digs himself in & it takes a hell of a lot to shift him. It's usually a case of last round, last man with him. In three months' intensive fighting we have captured less than a hundred POW, yet his casualties have been heavy & out of all proportion to ours. At least ten thousand dead Japs have been counted around Imphal, & his total dead on this front amount to not less than twenty thousand.

I wonder what the fighting in Normandy portends? Let's hope it won't be long now before the Bosche is hustled out of Jersey & Guernsey. What a day that will be for poor old Mummy. Pity we can't be there. There's a faint chance I may get three months' leave to England sometime this year as a certain amount of Indian Army officers are being allowed home – but the prospects are very remote as there are so many others who have been out here much longer without leave.

The situation on the Burma front is still confusing. The good thing is the opening of the road between Dunapur & Imphal. The Jap at last was beaten at Kohima & is now in full retreat. To the south of Imphal he is still full of fight & there's no knowing what mad scheme he might be up to next. The battalion has had some hectic fighting & in the last month or so has killed at least five hundred Japs, besides knocking out nine tanks. One of our rifleman has been put up for a VC – although badly wounded three times he destroyed three tanks on his own with a PIAT.

With fresh troops now coming in we are all hoping to be pulled out for a rest & some leave in the near future. Unlike you blokes in Italy we have no amenities to ameliorate the conditions, which since the monsoon started have been perfectly bloody. The whole place is flooded & we live in a sea of mud & slime.

Well, all the v best. Hope you are fit.

Yours, Malcolm

Last letter from Malcolm – written the day before he was killed

1st/7th Gurkha Rifles, 16 ABPO, 25 June 44

Dear old Dick,

Your and Fluffy's very welcome letters of 6 June arrived two days ago. I was so sorry to hear about poor little Richard; he seems to be going through a trying time & the heat in Chindwara is no doubt a contributory cause. Poor Fluffy – what rotten luck for you. What with the heat & no transport to get about, you must be regretting you ever married into the army! Oh well, all bad times must come to an end sometime or other, & then we shall all be able to make up for it. Actually it's not exactly a picnic up in these parts. The rains are now in full blast, and the whole of the Imphal plain is a sea of mud & slime. Conditions in our sector are unpleasant in the extreme. With the water rising at its present rate it's difficult to see how we can remain in our present positions. All our bunkers are flooded and casualties have to be evacuated by boat. During the other night the floods rose & simply washed me out of my bunker; it was too dark to see anything & next morning I discovered most of the blankets & such kit that remained to me had been swept away & most of our Mess had also gone. The numerous corpses which we had spent

*so much labour in burying had been washed up again,
& the whole place became disgusting. For some time I
had been having troubles of the usual sort, and a good
many other British Officers were in the same plight. Our
only latrine became a target for Jap snipers, so I had to
give up the unequal struggle & go to hospital for a few
days. In hospital I revelled in cleanliness & comfort.
It was heavenly to have a decent bath & lie on a bed
with white sheets. In our ward there were two order-
lies – twin brothers as like as two peas called George
& Cyril. I could never tell them apart, & for some days
thought they were the same person until I was told that
George was on duty during the day & Cyril at night!
They put me on a diet of Epsom's salt for four days, then
when I felt as empty as a drum, I was filled up with white
pills, as many as twenty to thirty a day, & soon became
completely bunged up. These pills acted like cement &
I now feel like a block of concrete! I expect I shall soon
be restored to my former condition once I start drinking that foul water again. It must be saturated with mi-
crobes – caused no doubt by the corpses which float
around! The ward is full of British Officers all suffering
from the same distressing complaint.*

*The situation here is improving although there are
still a lot of Japs milling around on the hills. The Japs
found Kohima too much for them, & after a rapid advance by our troops, contact was established between
our forces moving south from Kohima & troops moving
north. As a result the road is now open, & fresh troops
& supplies are now moving in. This I hope will mean
that we shall get some beer & whisky soon – things
which we haven't enjoyed for quite a long time.*

*To the south of Imphal the Japs have been rein-
forced & have been giving a lot of trouble. I wouldn't
be surprised should they attempt to raid Imphal itself
or lay a roadblock somewhere between Imphal & Bish-*

41

enpur. Wilfred Oldham, CO 1st/4th & one of the most brilliant soldiers in these parts, came to an untimely end last week. He rather rashly went out with a patrol into the hills & while crossing a nullah was killed by a sniper. He was only thirty-two or thirty-three & would probably have succeeded to command of a brigade very soon. He was a very brave fellow & had been wounded thrice since December. Casualties among COs have been heavy. Sammy Wingfield of 1st GR, Outram of the 5th, Marshall of 12th FFR [Frontier Force Regiment] and now Oldham have all been killed within the last month or so. A rather peculiar situation has arisen in the 1st/7th. Basil McDowell returned to us a week or two ago & took over command. Now Jim Robertson, who was wounded in the roadblock show last month, has returned. He is the pukka CO but McDowell is five or six years his senior. As two 2 i/cs couldn't be allowed, I have been or will be when I get out of hospital sent as temporary 2 i/c of the 2nd/5th which is now commanded by Philip Townsend. It's rather annoying being switched around like this – & need never have happened if Basil McDowell had not been recalled. I was just beginning to know the British officers & men in the 1st/7th & will now have to start all over again. However, I gather it is only temporary until McDowell is sent back to the 4th/7th. Meanwhile the 4th are without a CO & John Eustace, 2 i/c of our brigade, has gone to command them. This switching around of British officers is happening right & left, but I'm certain it's a bad thing for the battalions concerned. However good a British officer is, a battalion naturally resents a stranger coming in over the heads of all the other officers.

Young Nigel appears to be getting married on 24th – & referred rather mysteriously in his letter that he might be seeing my girlfriend Connie Lailey in the near future. If so that means he will be going to New York. Lucky beggar!

With things going as they are in Normandy I won't be surprised to see the Hun scuttling out of Jersey very soon. Marvellous if that does happen!

Well, no more for the present.
All the best & all my love.

Malcolm

Letter from the Brigade Deputy Commander to Dick

Col N Eustace, c/o HQ 17 Light Division, 16 ABPO

My dear McGill

I write to offer you my deep sympathy, and no less that of all ranks of the 1st/7th and 2nd/5th GR on the sad death of your brother. I had not known him for very long, but we were together for a short time in the 1st/7th when I came in as CO for a few days, and later when I was with the 2nd/5th, taking the place of Philip Townsend when he was wounded, your brother came over actually only the evening before he was killed. But to know him for however short a time was to like him; it was easy to see the regard in which he was held, and in the short time we were together his advice and help were of the greatest assistance to me. At the time of his death we were out on a day's operations. Your brother was sitting between me and Gouldsbury, the Adjutant, and we were in what we thought was defiladed ground. Without warning a shell arrived, one of several, and pitched amongst us, causing in all I think about a dozen casualties, killed and wounded. Your brother was hit in the head. He rolled over unconscious and it was at once evident that the wound was mortal. He died within about half an hour on the way to the Advance Dressing Station, or almost at once after arriving there – and was buried nearby and his grave registered. From the moment he was hit he cannot have known anything about it. I am afraid that is all I can tell you, except to add our deep sympathy in your loss, which we feel very greatly in the two units and in the whole brigade. The 1st/7th GR are dealing with his effects and formalities as he had only just arrived over with the 2nd/5th the evening before. I feel I have lost a friend, and the Army and the Gurkha Brigade an officer who upheld the highest traditions. I myself am on the move to some other job, at present un-specified. But letters to the above address will, I hope, be forwarded and if there is anything I can help over, I hope you will let me know.

Yours sincerely,

N Eustace

Letter to Dick from Lt Col Jim Robertson, CO 1st/7th GR

1st/7th Gurkha Rifles, c/o No 16 ABPO, 18 July 44

Dear McGill,

I am writing to you on behalf of myself and all ranks of the regiment to say how very sorry we were to hear about poor old Malcolm and to offer you our very sin-cere sympathy.

Malcolm, as you probably know, joined the regiment in Tiddim just before I arrived and throughout the time we were together he did all he possibly could to help me and I couldn't have had a more loyal supporter. When I was wounded he took over command and did extremely well bringing the battalion back through a pretty sticky period. When I got back here I found him in hospital with tummy trouble and when he was there he was posted to the 5th Gurkha Rifles as second in command as they were very short of British Officers. When Malcolm came out of hospital he joined the 5th up on a track where they were getting a good deal of shelling, and the day he arrived Malcolm was killed by an almost direct hit which also killed six men in their HQ. It upset me a lot when I heard about it as I had got to know Malcolm pretty well and we got on excellently together. All his effects are being sent to Second Echelon who, I presume, will get in touch with you. At any rate I will ask them to do so. I would be very grateful if you could let me have your mother's address, as I would like to write to her. Please write and let me know if I can be of any help to you over Malcolm's affairs and I would again like to offer you our very deepest sympathy.

Yours sincerely,

J R Robertson

Letter to Dick from Basil McDowell, 2 i/c 1st/7th GR

1st/7th Gurkha Rifles, 16 ABPO, 19 July 44
My dear Dick,

Thank you so much for your letter dated 7 July. Jim Robertson has written to you with all the details of the various questions you ask regarding Malcolm's death & his effects, & there is nothing for me to refer to except personal matters.

I was CO for ten days or so & Malcolm was my 2 i/c. I think we got on famously, and it was indeed a shock when we heard the bad news of his death. I think

I was the last person of this battalion to see him alive. He came up in a jeep from hospital where he had been for a few days and I met him on the road on his way up to his new battalion. We exchanged grouses and he went off. He often spoke to me about you and he seemed very fond of you.

Jim is attending to his affairs here but anything I can do in any way, you have but to ask.

I'm damned sorry about it all & you have my sympathy.

 Goodbye
 Yours ever
 Basil McDowell

Letter from Connie Lailey (Malcolm's girlfriend) to Jerry on hearing of Malcolm's death

275 Russell Hill Road, Toronto, Canada, 24 September 1944

Dear Jerry,

It was so thoughtful of you to write to me about poor Malcolm's death. It has been a great blow to me and I am terribly grieved for you and your brothers. I was very fond of him, as you know, and despair of ever meeting again so fine a person. His letters were always so brave and uncomplaining, & yet one could tell that he was having a perfectly rotten time. He had enough bad luck, goodness knows, without this final tragedy. I have been very unhappy since I heard the sad news and know how hard it must be for you and how dreadfully you must miss him. Your brother Nigel was in New York in August and first broke the news to me. I was so glad to meet him but oh – if it had only been under happier circumstances. He reminded me so much of Malcolm and it was almost more than I could bear. Don't you think he looks very like him? I hope I shall be able to see him again when he comes back to New York in November. He is very nice, isn't he – just like all the McGills.

I remember you much more than 'vaguely' and shall never forget those wonderful days in Jersey. I hope you will be back there soon and that you will find your mother well. It shouldn't be long now. But how different it will be. How one could wish it possible to turn the clock back five years and wipe out all that has happened in between. I am in Toronto now on a few weeks' vacation but must leave again for New York next week. I am working for Time Magazine there and am finding my work very interesting. I was in the Battlefronts section for some time and followed your exploits in Italy with great keenness. I hate to think what you are all going through while we sit in ease here at home; pray God it may all be over soon.

Do let me hear from you from time to time. I should hate to lose touch with the McGills. There are so few people to whom I can talk about Malcolm and I shall always be fond of Malcolm's brothers.

Good luck and God bless you,
Yours, Connie

Connie in Jersey in 1939 – shortly before the war.

A War Cemetery some thirty miles north of Rangoon, one of three which commemorate those lost in the Burma Campaign. Although his name is listed under 9th Gurkha Rifles, Malcolm's remains are not in this cemetery. They remain where he was buried when he died.

Photo taken by Christoph Kohler

In March 1944 Malcolm McGill was wounded in the jungle fighting, but returned to the front after two months' convalescence at Imphal. He was temporarily attached to another Gurkha battalion, which had been continuously engaged in terrific fighting for nearly four months. On 26 June it was attacking a strongly held Japanese position south west of Imphal, and McGill was in the Command Post when a Jap shell scored a direct hit. He was mortally wounded in the head and died half an hour later. Age thirty-three. A fine fellow, straightforward and fearless, an officer worthy of the splendid troops he led, by whom he was greatly beloved.

Extract from Victoria College's Book of Remembrance for those from the College who gave their lives in the Second World War

Malcolm's medals:
1939–45 Star, Burma Star, War Medal 1939–45.

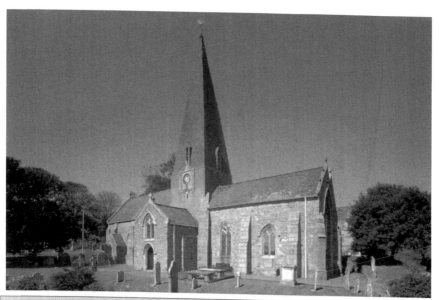

There is a memorial in St Clement, Jersey, dedicated to those from the parish who were killed during the First and Second World Wars.

Above – St Clement's Parish Church
Below – the memorial.

Photos taken by Rev David Shaw

6

DICK

Lieutenant Colonel R P T (Dick) McGill DSO
Born 1 July 1912 in Mussoorie, India. Died 1 September 1971 in Salisbury, Rhodesia (now Harare, Zimbabwe).

Commissioned from Sandhurst into the Indian Army in 1932 and attached to the 1st Battalion the Duke of Cornwall's Light Infantry before joining the 1st Battalion 8th Gurkha Rifles (1st/8th GR) in November 1933 &, subsequently, 2nd/8th GR in 1936 where he became Adjutant for four years until 1940, serving on the North-West Frontier. Instructed at the Small Arms School, Sangor, for eighteen months before marrying Frances in January 1942 and attending the Staff College in Quetta (with Malcolm). Posted to East Africa Command as an operations staff officer for a year from September 1942 and then to 14th Indian Jungle Division (part of 15th Corps, 14th Army) until November 1944 as a Grade 2 and Grade 1 training staff officer. Posted to 2nd/8th GR in Italy, as 2 i/c for a month before becoming CO in January 1945. The battalion, along with 2nd/6th & 2nd/10th GR, was part of 43rd Gurkha Independent Lorried Infantry Brigade in the Eighth Army advancing up the east coast of Italy along the Adriatic coast and inland over the Appenines, across a succession of rivers and ridges. Wounded in his bladder and groin in March 1945, after the River Senio crossing, by a mortar shell which hit his jeep, killing his driver and signaller, he rejoined his battalion in time for the battle across the Rivers Sillaro & Gaiano in April. In July 1945 the battalion embarked at Trieste, arriving in Tripoli in August. Appointed acting Brigade Commander until October but resumed his post as CO 2nd/8th in December 1945 once back in India. Awarded DSO for gallant & distinguished services in Italy. Reverted to 2 i/c 2nd/8th from December 1946 & reappointed as CO in September 1947. Retired from the Army in October 1947. His last few months in the Army were spent attempting to keep the peace between the Sikhs, Hindus and Muslims during the partition between India and Pakistan. He had three children: Richard, born 1942; Ian, born 1946; Julia, born 1948.

Although my father Dick was very happy as a soldier, he was initially keen to become a doctor but my grandfather reluctantly told him that he could not afford to pay for his medical training. He suggested (perhaps directed!) that Dick should sit for the Sandhurst entrance exam instead. This he duly did, subsequently leaving the College with the following short report from his company commander in 1932: *Cheerful and self-confident. He has worked hard and made a reliable corporal this term. His powers of leadership should develop still further with age. Keen on games. He should make a good officer. Graded above average on ability and average on leadership.*

Commissioned into the Indian Army, Dick spent his first year in India as a platoon commander with the 1st Battalion the Duke of Cornwall's Light Infantry before moving to 1st/8th Gurkha Rifles as a company commander in late 1933 and then to 2nd/8th Gurkha Rifles as Adjutant in 1936. Most of his service before and in the initial stages of the War was on the NW Frontier of India, in what is now Pakistan.

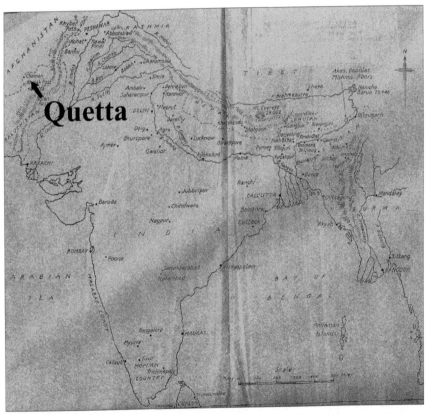

Map taken from page 1 of The History of the 8th Gurkha Rifles 1824–1949, compiled by Lieutenant Colonel H J Huxford OBE.

Quetta (arrowed) suffered a major earthquake in 1935 – described in a letter from Dick to his parents.

Quetta, Baluchistan. 6 June 1935

My dearest Mother and Father,

Last Monday, I scribbled a hasty chit to you which I hope you received O.K. Please let me know whether you got my cable which I dispatched to you a few hours after the catastrophe. By now you will have read the newspapers with their graphic accounts of the recent earthquake disaster up here. A lot of the information is incorrect, but quite a lot of it is true. To believe the actual facts one really has to come to Quetta and see things with one's own eyes.

I could write volumes telling you all what I have been through, which compared to what some others have been through is a mere nothing. Still, I can admit that I have seen and been through every phase of the whole show. A greater tragedy could not have befallen a place in quite so short a space. The big shock, which incidentally was the first one, came without a hint of any warning whatsoever at 0308 hours on 31 May. Everyone was fast asleep at the time. This was the unfortunate part, and accounts largely for the appalling loss of life. Most people in cantonments were sleeping out of doors, otherwise the loss amongst the military might have been heavier. Anyway the first shock did the damage: in ten seconds the whole bazaar and city were down and in shambles. A severer shock could seldom, if ever have been recorded in the history of earthquakes. The whole ground literally swayed at an incredible angle. I was jerked out of bed and could not move so paralysed with fright was I. I imagined I was in the throes of a bad nightmare or else the end of the world had come. The bungalow, however, strange to relate, did not come down, although it is badly damaged and quite unfit to live in. This applies to most buildings in cantonments, except the Air Force lines, which came down like a pack of cards, killing and wounding most of the personnel.

At the time, therefore, I never for a minute imagined that the shock had caused such a terrific lot of damage. Within half an hour, however, I was to find out. The troops were standing to and by 0345 we were down in the civil lines pulling people out of the debris. The civil lines including the Residency were completely flat. The loss of life here was appalling. Practically every bungalow contained a corpse. The part of the cantonment adjoining the civil lines was also in a bad way, and all the military mentioned in the papers as dead or wounded lived here. From 0410 to 0930 hours we were rescuing Europeans in this area, and had cleared most of the buildings at the end. In some cases, however, we were six hours in getting some people, some of whom were alive and kicking.

In the meantime we learnt that the whole bazaar and city containing over sixty thousand souls was absolutely flat, and that fires were raging all over the place. Every unit was given a certain area of the city to clear, and we were given what was perhaps the most densely populated part. Never do I want to see such a ghastly and awful spectacle as long as I live. Those Indians who had escaped were too shattered to help themselves, and the military were in sole charge. Hour after hour until late that night, we did nothing but dig for bodies. Strange to relate, we rescued any number of people. The same work went on for the next three days. We pulled out thousands of bodies and saved several hundreds. Eventually, however, the doctor forbade us to contin-

ue, as it was becoming notoriously unhealthy. We had been working in respirators but even so the odour was appalling. The city and bazaar, therefore, were closed and sealed by the troops. No one was permitted to enter. Even now there are cordons of troops all round the bazaar and all principle roads are piquetted. In the meantime the military had opened a refugee camp on the Race Course, which now contains over twenty thousand people, all Indians. Here the poor wretched people who had lost their all were cared for and given tents and rations. From here they were evacuated to India by trains all regulated by troops. Six trains leave daily each containing five hundred people.

Both the British Medical Hospital and the Indian Medical Hospital were flooded out with injured, as many as five thousand being admitted to the latter in three days. Of course, the chaos here was indescribable. The medical staff could not compete with it, and people lay for three days without even being attended to, so numerous were the injured.

The Mission Hospital and the Civil Hospital came down, and 90% of the patients there were killed. In fact, if it was not for the military, God alone knows what would have happened. General Karslake, who has organised the relief, deserves every bit of credit and praise due to him. The troops too were marvellous. They worked nonstop for three days and even now are working sixteen out of the twenty-four hours. The wives and daughters, too, of officers, have been splendid. Every one of them volunteered immediately to help at the hospitals, and now about three hundred of them have been enrolled into VADs. [Voluntary Aid Detachments] *Mind you, some of them are girls of seventeen and eighteen, and had never seen death before. Yet in one hour they saw perhaps death in all forms, so ghastly was the tragedy which had just been enacted. Of course, doctors and nurses have been coming up from all over India by air and train daily, and by now things are more or less in order. Even so the IMH still has four thousand injured. The others have either died or have been evacuated to the refugee camp on the Race Course.*

Of course, as you know, martial law is still in force. Everywhere the military are in control. Every troop is engaged in some sort of work. We are salvaging bungalows in that part of the cantonment area, which was badly affected. For three days now we have been working for twelve hours a day on salvage work and evacuating the wretched occupants and their salvaged goods to safer areas. The 2nd/8th are running the refugee camp. Several battalions are piquetting the city, others are collecting cattle and crops. The Signals have done marvellous work, and have been entirely responsible for all the communications. Sappers, too, have been marvellous, and have carried out grand work and so on and so forth. Mind you, we have several things to be thankful for: (a) That it was the city and not the cantonment which was raised to the ground; (b) That it was summer and not winter; (c) That such an able man as General Karslake is in charge.

At present everyone is living in tents. Another stroke of luck is that the railways are capable of sheltering two whole Divisions, some forty-five thousand people. I gather we will now live in tents for at least a year if not more. All women and children are being evacuated. I understand now the present area may be evacuated by the troops. We may move to Channan, which incidentally was not affected. The trouble at present is the fear of cholera and disease. Still, we must now rely on the medical and our own common sense to fight all disease.

Every shop, cinema, club, etc. is literally non-existent. In fact, Quetta as hitherto known does not exist. Except for a few hundred cantonment bungalows and both Generals' residents, every single house in the city is no more. You cannot honestly conceive what an appalling tragedy the whole place has witnessed. The future of Quetta will indeed be interesting. At present I cannot tell you anything although I have heard numerous rumours.

Now look here, Mummy and Daddy, one thing I entreat of you – please don't worry. I am O.K. and perfectly fit, although very weary. Please don't believe everything the papers say. True we are still having tremors and I gather we have to expect them for at least four or five months. Anyway, please don't worry.
Must stop now. Lots and lots of love.

Your loving son, Dick

Scenes from the Quetta Earthquake

Kandhari Bazaar from Bruce Road end

Kabari Market

The Quetta Club

Refugees queuing for accommodation

Wounded at the Military Hospital

A funeral pyre for Hindus near Galbraith Spinney. The ashes of a former one are in the foreground

Refugees at the Race Course

After the Quetta earthquake, Dick was engaged on operations in Waziristan and based for much of the time at Wana.

On taking over as Adjutant, Dick recalled his initial interview with the CO (Lieutenant Colonel Geoffrey Scoones – later General and Commander IV Corps in Burma). The CO told him, 'Look here, McGill, there are two types of officers as far as I'm concerned; the inefficient buffoon or the efficient sh-t. I'm an efficient sh-t – Got that!' Despite this introduction, Dick thoroughly enjoyed all his service with the battalion and found the mix of operations, sport and social life exhilarating. He worked and played hard – and thrived.

North-West Frontier Scenes

2nd/8th Gurkha Rifles in Wana, Waziristan 1938. Dick was Adjutant and Jerry was commanding Signal Troop in the Wana Brigade, at the same time.(Chris Yeates, C Company Commander on bicycle – later CO of the battalion and Dick took over from him in Italy)

Dick (left) with a brother officer

Above: A Wana column coming across the bridge over the Wana Toi in June 1938

The Battalion marching from Tiarza to Torwam

The Brigade Transport

Some of the troops at Torwam

A machine-gun post

Armoured Car column

Support from Mountain Gunners

And playing Polo at Wana in 1938

Dick (left) at a New Year's Ball in 1935 in Quetta

Dick with the Battalion Boxing Team

After his time as adjutant of his battalion, Dick enjoyed instructing at the Infantry School in Sangor, but was keen to get involved with the war and was therefore relieved to be selected for the Staff College at Quetta and subsequently posted on operations in East Africa, Burma and Italy. He did well at Staff College, being graded 24th out of 113 in the Order of Merit and with a promising report:

> *Pleasant and cheerful personality. A useful officer. Hardworking, reliable and loyal. Has qualities of leadership and strength of character. Quick, receptive brain. Logical. Judgement sound. Capacity for detail. Best in a 'G' (operations) appointment, either in the field or in a big office but suitable also in a training appointment. Slight but fit and wiry.*

Dick married Frances on 27 January 1942 and both Malcolm and Jerry managed to attend the wedding. My father saw more of my mother in the first six months of their marriage, while on the Staff Course, than he did for the next five and a half years on a series of deployments – until they moved to Rhodesia after he left the Army in late 1947. His first posting as a staff officer was to East Africa, based in Nairobi. He then served in Burma before rejoining his battalion in Italy.

Dick's wedding

Seated: Sir Henry Holland, Blanche and Cecil Tyndale-Biscoe, Patsy Dixon
Standing: Malcolm, Dick and Frances, Malcolm Dixon, Jerry

Frances (also known as Fluffy) was a widow whose first husband, Alec Best, had been killed in a riding accident before the war. She was the daughter of Canon Cecil Tyndale-Biscoe, a remarkable missionary and schoolteacher in Kashmir for fifty-seven years. She and Dick married in Lahore Cathedral, Punjab, on 27 January 1942. Richard was born ten months later on 22 November

Frances' Parents: Cecil and Blanche – married in 1891 in Kashmir

*Cecil on the Dal Lake near
Srinagar – very different from his
rowing at Cambridge where he
coxed the winning boat in 1884
against Oxford*

Blanche

Description of Dick's service in Italy while CO 2nd/8th GR, under command of 43rd Independent Gurkha Lorried Infantry Brigade – extracted from pages 189–200 of the History of the 8th Gurkha Rifles 1824–1949, compiled by Lieutenant Colonel H J Huxford OBE

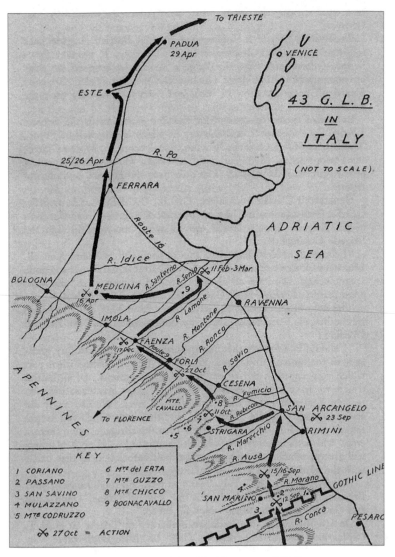

Map copied from Map No 13 at page 197 from
History of the 8th Gurkha Rifles 1824–1949

The ground was now clear for the final offensive of the war in Italy, and the 43rd Gurkha Lorried Brigade withdrew to rest and to train for their part in that great operation. The Germans had fallen back to prepared positions on the line of the Senio. Until 9 February 1945 the Battalion was, with the other two battalions of the 43rd Gurkha Lorried Brigade, engaged in reconnoitring, preparing and digging a brigade defensive position between the Lamone and Montone rivers. This was to foil a possible German attempt to cut the Eighth Army lines of communication east of Faenza.

On 12 January 1945 Dick took over command of the Battalion from Lieutenant Colonel Chris Yeates. On 10 February 1945 the 43rd Gurkha Lorried Brigade was placed under command of the 56th (London) Division. This Division was holding a sector opposite the River Senio, of which the brigade occupied a position near the town of Bagnacavallo and astride Route 16, the main Adriatic highway. The Brigade held a front of five thousand yards confronting intricate and elaborate defences with all three battalions being forward. The frontage of the battalion on the 43rd Brigade right was some 2,300 yards with three companies up and one company in reserve. On the Battalion's left were 2nd/6th Gurkha Rifles; on its right was the 1st Canadian Division. The river banks in winter commanded the flat, bare fields, over which the attack had to approach for at least a mile. A deep apron of mines and booby traps was sown along their front, and each of the four slopes of the river banks – two inner, two outer – had been fortified with wire and weapon pits, and cunningly contrived strong points. Tunnels ran through the banks for communication and protection, and they (the banks) had been broken in places in order that, if necessary, the approaches might be flooded.

Flame-throwing vehicles and manual flame-throwing equipment were brought forward to overcome this very strong obstacle. Artillery from 23rd Field Regiment was skilfully deployed so as to enfilade the inner side of a bank, whilst the Gurkhas held the outer bank. From 11 to 22 February 1945 the enemy positions were 'softened up' with artillery, battalion mortars and the Brigade machine-gun support group keeping the Germans busy. The Brigade was supported by a squadron of tanks, firstly from 11th Canadian Armoured Regiment (Calgary Regiment), and then from 2nd Royal Tank Regiment. Battalion patrolling was determined, locating no fewer than forty-eight Spandau posts by 20 February. In some cases patrols even succeeded in reaching the top of the riverbank in spite of wire, mines and squelching mud. The enemy responded and, with perfect observation posts on the bank, his artillery and mortar fire was accurate. The Battalion suffered casualties, noticeably in 'A' Company on the right. On two successive days 7 Platoon lost a complete section from heavy and accurate shelling. The date for the assault was drawing near, and 'B' and 'C' Companies were relieved, and brought back to the River Lamone for a rehearsal. This was made more realistic, as the enemy shelled the area with long-range artillery. The intention was to attack on the night 22/23 February, and to establish posts along the eastern bank of the River Senio, thus dominating the river, and preventing the enemy reinforcing his garrisons on the western bank. The plan was for 56th (London) Division with 43rd Gurkha Lorried Brigade (under command) to capture the east bank south of the railway, with forward troops right to left – 2nd/8th, 2nd/6th, 2nd/10th and 167th Infantry Brigade. North of the railway line the Canadian Division would support the attack by fire only.

The Battalion plan placed three companies forward: 'B' Company right, 'C' Company left, 'A' Company and Carrier Platoon holding the right flank from the railway line to 'B' Company's right. In reserve was 'D' Company. Surprise was essential; therefore until 'H' hour only normal harassing fire was maintained. From 'H' hour onwards fire was greatly increased by 25-pounder guns brought into 'silent' positions the day before, and enfilading the river line. The Battalion's 3-inch mortars under Lieutenant Baldwin played an important part in this fire plan and were in action continuously from 'H' minus one to 'H' plus four hours and then more or less continuously for the following ten days.

At 2100 hours on 22 February 1945 the attack began. For the rest of the night it was a race against time to get the forward platoons well consolidated, well supplied with ammunition, and well established with good communications. All dug furiously, roofing their scanty niches so that bombs, rolled over the top of the bank, might trundle by. Manual flame-throwers were rushed up and emplaced and individual cover enlarged into weapon pits. Supplies were brought up under heavy shellfire. Grenade expenditure was enormous (two thousand expended before dawn) and each section required (and received) about twenty-eight boxes. The signallers did splendid work, as they always did. First light on 23 February found the forward platoons well dug in. It was a fine achievement and successful beyond all expectations. At 1000 hours on 23 February the enemy attack began, with the first assault thrown against the battalion. Until 3 March the battle continued. Saps were driven up to the tip of the bank; tunnelling and counter-tunnelling went on. In this work, with its attendant raids, the Gurkha seldom came off second best. One party of 'C' Company digging through the bank ran into a German party, similarly engaged. Six enemy prisoners were taken belonging to the 98th Fusilier Battalion. Prisoners from this battalion stated that in three weeks on the Senio, 80 per cent of their fighting personnel had become casualties.

On 26 February a particularly determined attack was made by the enemy on a point known as the Bastion on the Battalion's sector. An intense mortar and artillery shoot crashed on the troops holding the position; adjacent earthworks collapsed, burying part of the garrison. Stroke and counter-stroke followed for the possession of this strong point. The gallantry of Subadar Jitbahadur Gurung (later awarded the Indian Order of Merit) and his platoon (13 Platoon) deserve special mention. From the night 23/24 February, for about one week, this platoon broke up attack after attack in the Bastion area. Often out of touch, short of ammunition, food and sleep, they put up a magnificent performance and remained aggressive until relieved. Until 3 March the fight went on before the battalion was relieved, actually dealing with two enemy attacks on 'D' Company sector whilst relief was in progress. So ended the battle of the Senio River. After nineteen days of continuous and nerve-racking fighting the 43rd Gurkha Lorried Brigade handed over three miles of secure flood bank.

There were 131 casualties sustained during February, with 30 killed, 98 wounded and 3 missing. Decorations awarded for the Senio River operations were one Indian Order of Merit (IOM), one Indian Distinguished Service Medal (IDSM) and four Military Medals (MM).

Dick summed up the conduct of the battalion:

> *The nineteen days during which we were in this sector will always be remembered by all ranks of the battalion. For sheer dogged determination, individual initiative and cheerful enthusiasm it would be hard to better.*

This fighting on the flood banks was unique in many ways, quite unlike anything encountered in the past. A fitting tribute to the men was expressed in a letter from the Commander 56th (London) Division to the Brigade Commander:

The reputation of the Gurkha was well known to me in peace time, but it had not been my privilege previous to the Gothic Line actions to fight side by side with them. From the time I learned to know them at San Arcangelo and near Savignano I have always had the greatest confidence in any task they may be called upon to do. It was with great pleasure therefore that I learned that your Brigade was coming to serve under my command on the Senio in the early part of this year. The task we had facing the enemy on the line of the Senio was fraught with difficulties and problems, but no troops could look back on that phase of operations with greater pride and satisfaction than your Brigade. As you know, it was necessary to show a proper sense of aggression towards the Boche and to drive him out of the bund on our side of the river and to get ourselves in position there. This involved a number of bitter hand-to-hand engagements and the holding of the position in very close proximity to the enemy. The continuous grenade and small arms fighting threw a great strain on all ranks, but the Gurkha day by day proved his fighting qualities and his superiority over the Boche. The loyalty and determination which everyone showed on the bund in accordance with my express intention was a source of great pride and satisfaction to me personally, and I shall not easily forget the smiling faces and cheerful hearts I always found whenever I visited the battalions of your Brigade. I am sure that the cleaning up of the bund by your Brigade made the subsequent assault crossing by other formations possible, and your efforts were therefore a great contribution to the start of the great offensive.

On the night 3/4 March 1945 the Battalion arrived at Forli for rest and reorganisation. Owing to the heavy casualties in NCO ranks, no fewer than sixty-six promotions had to be made, and there were not sufficient lance-naiks to fill the naik vacancies.

On relief after the Senio battle, the 43rd Gurkha Lorried Brigade came under command of the 2nd Polish Corps; their sixth masters in six months of almost continuous fighting. Their role was to be a new one. The Brigade was given two armoured regiments (one of which was their old friends the 14th/20th Hussars), two Artillery Field Regiments, Armoured Troops Carriers known as Kangaroos and designated as the pursuit group of the 2nd Polish Corps. Up to 12 April 1945 the Battalion was engaged in occupying areas in relief of the 5th Battalion of the 2nd Carpathian Brigade and in intensive training to fit them to carry out their new role. Patrol activity took place, but no operations of any note occurred.

It was then decided that during the spring offensive the Brigade was to be lorry borne, supported by one field battery RA, one anti-tank troop RA and two squadrons of tanks. Following the clearing of the Senio on 11 April, the Polish Corps drove on to Bologna. The right flank was open, and the 43rd Gurkha Lorried Brigade hurried on to seize Medicina, an important crossroads, through which a counter-attack from the north might be launched. The Battalion led the way, and swept on to within three miles of the Sillaro River, encountering en route a network of canals and many river crossings which were impassable to wheels and tracks without previous bridging, while the infantry required boats (except in a few isolated cases).

There were delays and setbacks, but the 43rd Brigade drove on. Each battalion in turn did good work, and Medicina was captured after very heavy fighting in cellars, in lofts and even on the rooftops. German paratroopers formed the opposition and these tough fighters put up a desperate resistance. When dawn broke on 16 April, six captured guns, two captured tanks, one hundred shaken prisoners, and dead Germans everywhere were all that remained of the war in Medicina. In clearing the town, 'D' Company 2nd/8th assisted the 2nd/6th Gurkha Rifles, the battalion largely responsible for the capture. The tide of battle swept on to Gaiana, the next river obstacle. Here the Germans stood in strength, having brought from Bologna the 4th Paratroop Division. The 2nd/6th Gurkha Rifles, in a gallant attempt to sustain the momentum of the pursuit, threw themselves at the river, but the opposition was too strong, and a prepared full-scale assault was necessary.

The 2nd/8th gave much needed help to the 2nd/6th on 17 and 18 April, and 'A' Company actually succeeded in getting on the river bank at 0100 hours on 18 April, but had to be withdrawn after becoming too isolated, fortunately without a single casualty thanks to the effective artillery, mortar and air support laid on to get them off. On the afternoon of 18 April the New Zealanders came up on the right flank of the 43rd Gurkha Lorried Brigade and the Brigade once again came under the command of the 2nd New Zealand Division. On the night 18/19 April, the great attack, which was to provide the final blow to the enemy, was launched. The plan was to cross the Gaiana, two tributaries and a canal, with 9th New Zealand Brigade on the right and 43rd Gurkha Lorried Brigade on the left, as assaulting formations. This involved, in addition to the crossings, an advance of four thousand yards across unknown country in the pitch dark; a formidable undertaking, especially as the Battalion had been continuously in action for six days and nights. Confronting the advance were the 1st and 4th Paratroop Divisions, the cream of what remained of the German Army in Italy.

The 43rd Brigade attacked with 2nd/8th Gurkha Rifles on the right, 2nd/10th Gurkha Rifles on the left and 2nd/6th Gurkha Rifles in reserve.

The outline of the Battalion's attack, with one squadron 2nd Royal Tank Regiment in support, was:

Phase 1: To assault the Gaiana and the first tributary (Quaderna) with: Forward Companies: 'D' right, 'B' left. Support Companies: 'C' right, 'A' left.

Phase 2: To establish a bridgehead over the River Quaderna, and consolidate prior to a further advance to the second tributary (Idice) with: Forward Companies: 'C' right, 'A' left. Support Companies: 'D' right, 'B' left.

A tremendous barrage from the artillery (seventeen regiments) and all available tanks and mortars opened up at 2130 hours on 18 April 1945, a heartening sound to the assaulting troops. At 2150 hours 'B' and 'D'

Companies crossed the start line and advanced to within two hundred yards of the riverbank. Wasp flame-throwers opened up, throwing huge tongues of flame over the enemy's positions. 'B' and 'D' Companies charged the bank and for some ten minutes there were sharp hand-to-hand struggles. These companies were not to be denied, however, and, having captured thirty paratroopers, crossed the Gaiana and reached the next river (Quaderna) behind the barrage, thus bringing Phase 1 to a successful conclusion. At about 0100 hours on 19 April, 'C' and 'A' Companies passed through. They quickly met opposition and Lieutenant John Williams, who was leading 'C' Company, was mortally wounded. Despite this, the opposition was quickly overcome and first light saw the 9th New Zealand Brigade and the Battalion dug in on the Quaderna. The Battalion had also succeeded in capturing one bridge intact and consequently, shortly after first light, the supporting tank squadron came up to the forward companies. On the left flank of the Battalion, which was open, the enemy kept up a heavy fire and two small counter-attacks were repulsed by 'A' Company. Eventually a platoon of 'B' Company dislodged the enemy from some houses from which much of the firing had come. On the evening of 19 April, the Battalion was relieved by a battalion of the 5th New Zealand Brigade and moved to an area east of Medicina for much needed rest, after seven days of continuous action. Here a batch of reinforcements joined. This battle of the Gaiana was practically the end for the enemy in Italy. A hole had been punched for pursuit. The enemy never stood again.

The rest period lasted for two days only and on 22 April the Battalion moved forward again, crossing the River Po on 25–26 April. This was a long and trying business, there being only one pontoon bridge and much traffic. Rain made things worse by turning all the tracks into mud. From the Po, the New Zealanders and 43rd Gurkha Lorried Brigade drove on. It was rumoured that the enemy had withdrawn the bulk of his forces to the Venetian line just north of Este. Turning off from the main road to seize Este, the 43rd Brigade then raced for Padua. The New Zealanders were well on the road to Trieste and Austria. The Brigade had every hope of seeing the end from a front-line view, but it was not to be. Padua, reached on 29 April, was in a very lawless state. Fascists fought partisans and the town required a garrison. The 43rd Gurkha Lorried Brigade took charge and restored law and order. On 2 May the surrender of the German army in Italy was announced.

During the period 13 April–8 May, the battalion suffered another 100 casualties, with 31 killed and 69 wounded. Decorations gained in the same period were one DSO, two MCs, one MBE, one IDSM and one MM.

From the end of the war in Europe to the date of its embarkation from Italy, the battalion was visited by the C-in-C India (General Sir Claude Auchinleck), the GOC Eighth Army (Lieutenant General Sir Richard Creery), the GOC XIII Corps (Lieutenant General Sir John Harding), and the GOC 2nd New Zealand Division (Lieutenant General Sir Bernard Freyberg).

The 43rd Gurkha Lorried Brigade's associations in the campaign had been happy, but they may be pardoned for regarding the first and last of these associations with the 1st British Armoured Division and with the 2nd New Zealand Division as something especially close. To the Brigade, the 1st Armoured Division were always 'our tanks' and Sir Bernard Freyberg was 'our General'.

Tension in Trieste returned the 43rd Gurkha Lorried Brigade back under command of the New Zealanders for the last time. It was therefore a happy circumstance that the Brigade should be seen off by their old comrades on embarking. The bands of the New Zealand Division played off each battalion in turn and General Freyberg took the salute.

So ended active operations for the 2nd Battalion in the Second World War. General Sir Claude Auchinleck issued the following message at the close of his inspection of the Brigade Group:

> *I am delighted to have had this opportunity of seeing you all. I have never seen troops look fitter, or in better fettle. You have done magnificently. You are all obviously proud of yourselves, and with good reason. I wish you all Good Luck and God Speed.*

General Freyberg wrote to the Brigade Commander on 22 May:

> *I should like to take this opportunity to put on record my gratitude to you, and all under your command, for the distinguished part which you played in our recent*

successful operations. Of all battles which we have fought, there is none that gives greater satisfaction to New Zealanders than that of the Gaiana River. We had many old scores to settle with the 'Para boys' and the battle which you fought against them, side by side with our own 9th Brigade, gave them a crack which their survivors will not easily forget. New Zealanders will always remember with gratitude their association in that battle with the 43rd Gurkha Lorried Infantry Brigade. 'On behalf of the N.Z.E.F. I send to you, and to all ranks of your Brigade, our sincere thanks for all that you have done. Good Luck and God Speed in the times which lie ahead.

On 8 July the Battalion embarked at Trieste and disembarked at Haifa on 15 July, where they joined the 31st Indian Armoured Division. On 2 August the Battalion arrived at Tripoli, remaining there until January 1946, with leave being granted to as many as could be spared. At the end of January orders to return to India were received and most of the Battalion moved to Suez for embarkation, with an advance party moving overland from Syria, through Iraq, Persia, and West Baluchistan to Quetta. There the Battalion concentrated for reorganisation and leave. At the end of April the Battalion moved to Secunderabad, where, with the 2nd/6th and 2nd/10th Gurkha Rifles, the 43rd Gurkha Lorried Brigade was re-formed.

A 43rd Gurkha Lorried Brigade Sign

Dick had huge admiration and affection for his cheerful soldiers with their indomitable spirit

A break for a game of volleyball   *A Gurkha driver*

2nd/8th Gurkha Rifle Battalion Officers in Italy on VE Day
(Dick in centre of front row)

Dick's medals

DSO, NW Frontier 1937–39 Campaign Medal, 1939–45 Star,
Burma Star, Italy Star, Defence Medal, War Medal 1939–45

Copy of the Recommendation for Dick's award of The Distinguished Service Order

Award recommended by Brigadier A R Barker, Commander 43rd Gurkha Independent Lorried Infantry Brigade and endorsed by Lieutenant General R L McCreery, Commander 8th Army. Published in The London Gazette 13 December 1945, Entry 6074.

For gallantry, outstanding leadership and great tactical skill in battle.

Lieutenant Colonel McGill has commanded the 2nd Battalion, 8th Gurkha Rifles for the past five months. He took over a difficult task, but by his energy, contempt for danger, great tactical skill and magnificent example he has inspired his Battalion with new life and has produced outstanding results.

In the riverbank fighting on the River Senio 3637 in February 1945, Lieutenant Colonel McGill was faced by a determined and tenacious enemy, holding elaborate defences and strongly supported by artillery and mortars. By his cool skill, careful planning, tenacity and personal disregard of danger he secured and held against persistent counter-attack one and a half miles of the Eastern stop-bank.

In the advance to the River Sillaro 1714 on 14 April 1945, he led the brigade advance with his battalion. By his dash, initiative and fearlessness he quickly overcame sharp and determined enemy opposition and enabled the Brigade to form up quickly to the River Sillaro.

In the attack on the River Gaiano 0947 on 18/19 April he led his battalion against determined paratroopers of the 4th Parachute Division who had come fresh into battle and who were strongly dug in and supported. In a magnificent attack of bitter fighting the Battalion fought its way forward three thousand yards, crossed three major water obstacles, took over a

FOUR BROTHERS IN ARMS

hundred paratrooper prisoners and secured the battalion at 069499 intact. By first light on 20th April the battalion was ready to continue the advance. These splendid results were largely due to the inspiring leadership of Lieutenant Colonel McGill.

In all these actions and throughout the recent fighting the success of the 2nd Battalion 8th Gurkha Rifles has been largely due to the outstanding leadership, fearlessness and stirring example shown by Lieutenant Colonel McGill.

The Partition of India in 1947

The Viceroy, by now Lord Mountbatten who had succeeded Lord Wavell, reluctantly sanctioned the division of India into India and Pakistan. It had proved impossible to secure an agreement between Congress, led by Nehru and the Muslim League led by Jinnah. There were, inevitably, difficult problems concerning the boundaries between the new states, especially in the provinces of Punjab in the NW and Bengal in the east, which both contained many Muslims. The boundary award in Punjab cut through areas occupied by Sikhs, Muslims and Hindus who were all neighbours. At once a two-way exodus began, with Muslims moving west and Sikhs and Hindus moving east. Some six million Muslims migrated from Punjab to the new Pakistan and about 4.5 million Sikhs and Hindus to the areas between Amritsar and Delhi. In Bengal well over a million Hindus left the eastern sector (now Bangladesh), while thousands of Muslims from Calcutta and elsewhere sought shelter in east Bengal.

79

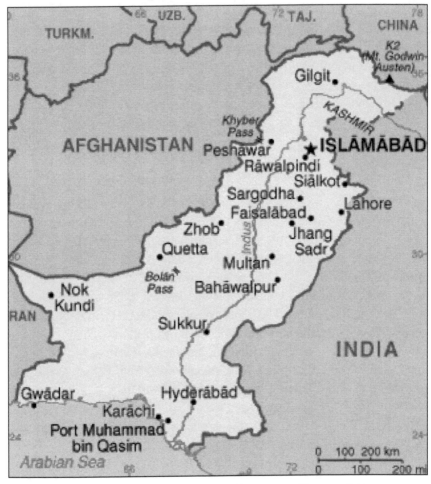

Map from the Univesity of Texas Online Collection – www.lib.utexas.edu/maps
Courtesy of the University of Texas Libraries, the University of Texas at Austin.

Pakistan is shown, between India and Afghanistan.
Kashmir still remains disputed territory.

Two letters from Dick to Jerry, written just before he left India, which highlight the terrible events surrounding the partition of India into India and Pakistan

Lahore, 5 Oct 1947

My dear Jerry,

It's the first time for ages I have an opportunity of writing. Heaven knows when there'll be another chance. Things are happening rapidly. I've had my marching orders and hope to be off any day. First though, I'm rushing up to Kashmir to collect Fluffy's parents. Kashmir is virtually isolated. I am going up in a military vehicle plus escort. From Lahore to Delhi one has to travel in convoy. The Sikhs are murdering British Officers and so far have killed about a dozen. From Delhi the old dears will go to Bombay and I will rush off to Madras to collect the family. Once in Bombay I am hoping that our passages to Rhodesia will materialise anytime in early Nov. One has to be on the spot these days. I hand over command of the Battalion temporarily to Joe Whyte. He has volunteered to extend his service until January. But by then we will be Indianised. The policy is to remove all British Officers by 31 Dec. So far we haven't one Indian Officer. Fantastic really but there it is. It's awful rushing off like this but this is no country now for a white man, let alone a white woman & family. I didn't tell you that Horace ratted & literally fled back to UK with sheer fright. That was on 2 Sep. He couldn't take the killing & corpses.

The Punjab business is simply ghastly. So far the estimate is ½ million killed since July. Mind you, when they indulge in a spot of killing it is pretty wholesale. Several refugee trains started last week but as many as

81

two thousand have been killed in each. A refugee foot column near Firozpur was attacked by Sikhs and had eight thousand killed. It's completely indiscriminate – many women & kids. Atrocities of the most horrible nature are being committed daily. I've seen the results of hundreds of such acts. In fact, I'm browned off with seeing mutilated corpses. Between Lahore & Amritsar on the Citi Road you will count up to three thousand corpses lying alongside the road. Cholera too in severe epidemic form is taking a heavy toll. In fact, it's sheer hell.

To add to our troubles we've had the worst floods for two hundred years. The Sutlej particularly, but also the Ravi & Beas. Firozpur has been wiped out & twenty thousand people believed drowned. Roads & railways all over have been destroyed. Next year there is bound to be a famine & millions will die. Refugees in their millions are on the move both from & to Pakistan. Troops have to escort the refugees of the minority community. 2nd/8th GR are engaged in looking after eight hundred thousand Sikhs emigrating from Lyallpur to Khem Karan & Ludhiana. It's a frightful job & so terribly exacting. Two platoons escort a party of thirty thousand! We have to guard them from being cut up as well as feed them & doctor them. Normally we lose about two hundred in each column per day, mainly through weakness & cholera. The Sikhs, though, on the Hindustani side are the buggers. They are very well organised into armed bands & knock hell out of Muslim refugee columns. The 1st/9th GR under Reilly escort Muslims from Jullundur to Lahore. So far the 1st/9th GR have shot more than three thousand Sikhs. We have shot about six hundred Muslims.

Unfortunately the Army (Indian Army) have behaved very badly. All Muslim troops naturally are pro

Pakistan & vice versa. Only the Gurkha Brigade under its British Officers remain impartial. There are now 8 battalions in the Punjab area – three in Pakistan & five in East Punjab. Everyone is shouting for Gurkhas. All Brit troops were withdrawn in July. What an awful mess. Normal unit administration has collapsed. I haven't heard from F [Fluffy] for ages. Letters & telegrams never turn up at all.

Sorry for this moan, but it's got me down. I only want you to realise how perfectly wretched & bloody the whole show is. It's bloody civil war. Never have I performed such remarkable duties as I have these past two months; from shooting looters to handling cholera corpses & bringing babies into the world. I haven't a clue what's happening outside the Punjab. Never see a paper or letter. If you write, address me c/o Lloyds, New Delhi. My Rhodesian address will be c/o Standard Bank of SA, Salisbury. I apologise for doing nothing but speak of what I'm doing.

I suppose you've started a new term now [Jerry instructing at Sandhurst]. England too seems to be heading for economic trouble & the future looks grim. No word from Mummy at all.

My love to you both. Yours ever

Dick

C/o Lloyds Bank, New Delhi, 11 Nov 1947

My dear Jerry,

A line to tell you that we are in Bombay awaiting our ship, the SS Tairea which is expected to sail for Beira on 19 Nov. It's thrilling to know that at long last we will soon be on our last lap. Fluffy's father & mother are with us. I managed to evacuate them from Kashmir on 10 Oct, shortly after all this trouble up there started. Thank heavens we succeeded in getting away safely. I don't suppose the home papers ever give much news as to what has been happening out here, but you can take it from me that present conditions in the North are quite chaotic – nothing functions whatsoever. Over one million folk [Dick's estimate] have been killed whilst cholera too has taken a fearful toll. In Lahore at one time there were six hundred deaths a day.

Apart from the Muslin & Non-Muslim refugee problem, which involves the mass migration of over fifteen million people, the Government is now concerning itself with the evacuation of Europeans. At one time conditions in the North were so bad that military convoys under British military escorts were laid on to evacuate all Europeans from Peshawar, Kashmir, Simla, Dharmsala, etc. Every ship leaving Bombay is full of evacuee families. India has long ceased to be a safe place for any lone European, though there are numerous folk who refuse to 'see the writing on the wall' & like to think nothing has changed. This is particularly so in the case of places like Madras & Bombay.

There will be no British officers in any of the six Gurkha regiments destined to go to the Indian Army (i.e. 1GR, 3GR, 4GR, 5GR, 8GR & 9GR) by 1 Dec. Things have been moving so rapidly that it was finally decided to Indianise as quickly as possible, irrespective of the consequences. You can just imagine what the outcome will be. I left the Battalion two weeks ago. There wasn't one Indian officer appointed then. It's an avalanche, which once started on its way will be unstoppable. Still, it's India's pigeon. Pakistan, on the other hand, is appealing for British officers and several hundreds have volunteered. Mind you, the terms are jolly good – full pay plus pension plus 300 rupees per month allowances. But, to be perfectly candid, any chap with a family out here would be mad to accept them. The risks are too great. If I was a bachelor I would probably stay. One could put up with a lot such as trains not running, aircraft failing to take off, unqualified doctors, corrupt & inefficient civil servants, black-market prices – not to mention complete & utter lawlessness. The days of the Nabobs have returned where fortunes can be made rapidly. I could have made several lakhs [a lakh is a hundred thousand rupees] in the Punjab riots helping to evacuate wealthy Indians. One man, Mr Moolchand, put fifteen thousand rupees in one thousand-rupee notes into my hand for helping him & was awfully hurt when I returned them!!! Still there it is. A number of Indian officers have made a packet, and I certainly knew of one British Officer who was in the habit of demanding bribes. Oh well, it was certainly a party whilst we were roaming around Pakistan. Life was full of interest, but I am thankful to have the experience behind me. Thank God Fluffy & the kids were safely ensconced in the Nilgiris. It was certainly a relief not to have them anywhere near the danger area.

It's a thrill to be setting out on a fresh venture. I can't help having regrets at having chucked the Army but, on the other hand, peacetime soldiering under present conditions doesn't appeal to me an awful lot. Time will tell whether I have been wise or not, but I am certain that life in the colonies has much to offer. Thank heavens they've given me one year's leave pending retirement on ¾'s major's pay, so it will give me a chance to look round for a job. I am sure there are lots of openings. For the first few months, however, I am going to do damn all except sit back & take it easy.

We've been given a house fully furnished until end of Feb, through Margaret Tyndale-Biscoe – a cousin-in-law of Fluffy's. By March I hope we've found some more permanent abode, either as paying guests on a farm or a rented house. I have actually purchased a four-acre building plot ten miles from Salisbury for the vast sum of £300. If all is well we will build a house for £2,500, but I don't want to spend so much from my gratuity. To start with, Fluffy's parents will be sharing the house with us until such time as Fluffy's brother Julian can take them in. It's all very exciting. I can't tell you how desperately anxious we are to have a settled home after our wanderings. The past year and more has been absolute hell in every way. Two hot summers under canvas (one in the Punjab) without any form of comfort or amenities at all. And above all, the constant moving at short notice. And as for the expense, I shudder to even contemplate what we've forked out in hotel bills & travelling. At the time of writing we're in Bombay paying £3 a day in a hotel. I see from The Times that over 1½ million people are waiting to emigrate from the UK. What I feel is that one can help the old country far more by going to a colony and doing a job of work in, say, producing more food, tobacco & what have you, rather than going home & trying to exist on the already meagre rations.

We often think of you & Joy & wonder how life is treating you. I suppose the RMA [Sandhurst] must be very interesting. I don't think you could be in a better job. What news of Margaret & Nigel? Has No. 2 arrived yet? What news of Mother? I haven't heard from her for ages. Will you please ask Thomas Cook to book her a passage by sea or air to Rhodesia for next autumn. We should have accommodation for her by then. She wants a change & six months out of England will give her a new lease of life.

Our love to you both – all the v best of luck. Write when you have time.

Yours aye, Dick

En route to Rhodesia

British India Steam Navigation Co. Ltd, SS TAIREA,
28 Nov 47

My dear old Jerry,

I haven't heard from you for literally ages, not that it means you haven't written because in India nowadays the postal service never functions. What a rush it's been too, getting things arranged. Collecting Fluffy's parents from Kashmir in the nick of time & then the family from the Nilgiris. We fetched up in Bombay & stayed in the Officers' Holiday Camp for a fortnight. There we met masses of folk all teed up to catch boats to every part of the Empire. It won't surprise you to hear that nearly 50% of the Europeans are going to South Africa, Australia, New Zealand and Rhodesia. No one wants to go home.

India is chronic. Complete anarchy in the North. There will be a war one day between India & Pakistan. Palachari [Sri Chakravarti Rajagopalachari] is to be the new Governor General in place of Lord Louis. The Sikhs have wangled to squeeze in everywhere & just you wait & see. There will be the most almighty bust-up very soon. Heaven help them.

This will have to be my Xmas letter to you both. It brings with it all our love & best wishes for a very happy Xmas.

All the best

Yours aye, Dick

7

JERRY

Brigadier A F (Jerry) McGill OBE
Born 20 October 1914 in Farnham, Surrey. Died 16 February 1998 in Crawley, Sussex.

Commissioned into The Royal Signals from Woolwich in 1934. Served in the India & Waziristan District Signals in the 1936–39 operations against the Faqir of Ipi (with Dick) and was Mentioned in Despatches. As Adjutant he assisted in raising 1st Indian Armoured Divisional Signals in 1940 & served as 2 i/c of that unit in Persia & Iraq. In 1943 he took command of 4th Indian Divisional Signals in the Middle East and saw them through the Italian Campaign, including the two battles of Cassino. He was awarded the OBE and was Mentioned in Despatches. In January 1945 he became Senior Instructor in the Regimental Wing at the School of Signals at Sandhurst. Some fourteen months later he attended the Staff College at Haifa for six months with his youngest brother Nigel, returning to Sandhurst in November 1946 as the Chief Instructor of the Signals Wing. From 1950–53 he was a Staff Officer in Malaya during the Malayan Emergency and was again Mentioned in Despatches. From 1954–55 he commanded 5 Corps Signal Regiment before being posted in 1956 to the War Office, London, in the Military Operations Directorate, being promoted to Colonel during his last six months there. In 1959 he joined Supreme Headquarters Allied Powers Europe (SHAPE), just outside Paris, as a Colonel on the General Staff responsible for Organisation & Training Policy for NATO Forces. In 1961 he was promoted Brigadier and posted as Commandant the Army School of Signals in Catterick, Yorkshire, for three years. From 1965–66 he was Chief of the Exercise Planning Staff at SHAPE, Paris, before spending his last six months in the Army negotiating with the Belgian authorities over the move of SHAPE to Brussels. He retired from the Army in 1967. During his military career he attended the Army Staff College in 1946, the RAF Staff College in 1949, the Joint Services Staff College in 1954 and the Imperial Defence College in 1964. Married Joy in April 1945.

Waziristan

Waziristan in 1937 was full of challenge and adventure for a young officer and Jerry relished his time there. He saw quite a bit of both Malcolm and Dick before the war and served alongside Dick in Wana for some of this period.

Waziristan 1937

Wana Pass under snow on 31 December 1937

Unit movement on foot on the North-West Frontier

Toikhulla Camp with a Rajput picquet

*Two tribesmen on
the Frontier*

Two letters from Jerry written in June 1940 to his parents at Bryn Y Mor in Jersey. The letters were returned to him, unread, due to the German occupation of the island.

Brigade Headquarters, Razmak, NW Frontier, India,
9 June 1940

I am sorry I missed writing last week but there has been an awful lot doing and I seem to have had no time at all. The last home letter received by me was sent by Dick, who at the same time gave me all his good news. It's a grand thought to think that Malcolm & Dick are now with each other in Shillong; they will have any amount to chat about before old Malcolm goes on to rejoin his regiment. I wish I could have got away on some leave to see them both.

How are you, Daddy? Have you left the dispensary now? I do hope you are feeling stronger and I bet Nigel's leave did you the power of good. I expect you are finding all this treatment and dieting very irksome, but it is worth it. And you, Mummy darling, thank you for your regular letters; in these difficult times I love getting them more than ever.

The recent war news has been none too cheerful and dear old England is taking some very hard knocks just now. The spirit at home now is marvellous and does really make one proud to be an Englishman. In spite of all our follies and lack of action during the past decade there is no doubt that the average Englishman is just as courageous as any of our forefathers and I know we'll beat these b— Huns in the end even if it means sacrificing everything. There's a tremendous desire among the average Indian to help and there is a feeling that the Government are doing a great deal of harm by not re-

93

ally expanding things in a big way out here. Anything to avoid the spending of money seems to be the matter.

Major Stevenson (whom you both know and have met in Jersey several times) is in Razmak now on a special job. He asks very warmly after you both and asked me specially to send his very best salaams to you. He says you have always been so good to his wife whenever she has been in Jersey.

Nigel appears to be loving his job. I'm very glad he is able to get occasional leave to see you; it must be a great comfort. He must be a hell of a hit now with his captaincy and his job of instructor. I shall definitely have to watch my step when I see him again and keep very quiet about our bow and arrow methods up here.

Dick's great friend Walter Walker of the 1st/8th GR [he later commanded the British Forces against Indonesia during the Borneo confrontation in the early 1960s and eventually became a four-star General commanding the NATO forces based in Norway] is at present officiating staff captain here and as such is living in the Brigade Mess. We are a very happy lot; due mainly to the spirit of Brigadier Dennys, a really grand man and tremendous fun. He plays games and runs about hills like a man half his age.

Do give my best wishes to any of my friends you may meet, some of them must be going through difficult and anxious times.

No more news. So cheers for the time being and God bless.

Your loving son

Jerry

Brigade Headquarters, Razmak,
16 June 1940

It was grand receiving welcome letters from each of you. They cheered me up tremendously; they'll probably be the last airmail ones I'll receive for a long time. I am not quite sure but think we'll have to rely entirely on the sea route around the Cape now – it takes at least five weeks from door to door. Still, it can't be helped.

Poor Col & Mrs Carey; they have my deepest sympathy. Tony was such a jolly good robust sort of chap. I had forgotten too that he was married; I feel very sorry for his young wife.

I didn't know that John Pendergast had gone home as a frontier warfare expert. I wonder what he'll be doing now that Norway has been evacuated? The news from Europe is most disturbing. Poor old France is going through hell at the hands of the German armies. My admiration for the French people is tremendous. At the present time France's prospects look pretty grim, but, who knows, Hitler may equally be reaching the end of his endurance. Today's news states that the French and Allied line will be again established on the Loire River. I wonder what is going to happen to the Maginot Line? I think it is a very good idea moving into a flat, provided you can make the necessary arrangements about the present house and also find a decent flat. It really would be worth it. Neither of you are as young as you used to be and Bryn Y Mor must be difficult to run now, especially during the present time. I hope that Mrs Le Sauvage succeeds in sub-letting Bryn Y Mor

There is a very strong feeling in India, especially among the younger people, both British & Indian, that the Government are being wet in not getting down to the war out here. Excuses of financial difficulties still carry far more weight with the average politician and civil officer than the obvious threat to the British Empire and India itself. I wonder how much longer we are going to sit tight out here.

Malcolm should be arriving in Landhi Kotal today. I wonder how he will like it after Burma. He will probably take time settling down to regimental soldiering again.

I was sorry to hear that dear Colonel Robertson had been so very ill. Poor Joan, I feel very sorry for her in many ways. She has money and many of the luxuries of life but she has never had any family life. The older I grow the more I appreciate our rather vigorous and eventful family life. Damned lucky having parents like you and brothers like Malcolm, Dick and Nigel. What more could anyone have wished for.

Hope you are both well and that you are stronger, Daddy. My love to all our friends, the Hultons, Douglases and Robertsons, etc.

Your loving son

Jerry

Jerry as a subaltern

With Dick in Quetta before the earthquake

While serving on the NW Frontier

In Italy after the Battle for Cassino

Copy of the Recommendation for Jerry's Award of the OBE, during the Italian campaign

Lieutenant Colonel McGill has throughout the almost continuous operations in which this Division has been involved from 1st May to end of August 1944, shown marked ability, powers of command and devotion to duty. The operations have on every single occasion comprised a pursuit of the enemy in face of opposition of varying intensity and very severe demolitions in country of a mountainous nature and most adverse to the maintenance of communications. That highly satisfactory communications have been maintained is due largely to Lieutenant Colonel McGill's technical knowledge, resourcefulness and drive. He has never spared himself or his men and they have always respected his leadership. The speed of controlled movements the Division has been able to maintain in such difficult country against opposition and often under very adverse weather conditions, has been largely due to Lieutenant Colonel McGill's efficient handling of the signal resources of the Division.

Recommended by Major General A W W Holworthy, Commander 4th Indian Division. Endorsed by Lieutenant General C F Keightley, Commander 5 Corps. Published in The London Gazette 17 April 1945, Entry 2068

Jerry's medals
OBE, NW Frontier Campaign Medal 1936–37 and 1937–39 Bar,
with Mention in Despatches Oak Leaf, 1939–45 Star, Africa Star,
Italy Star, Defence Medal, War Medal 1939–45 with Oak Leaf,
Malayan Campaign Medal with Oak Leaf.

Marriage to Joy on 9 April 1945 at Redhill   *Joy*

Jerry met Joy while on leave in London at the end of 1944 and staying with Nigel and Margaret who had themselves very recently married. She happened to be the sister of his Second-in-Command (Alan Pownall) and Jerry was instantly captivated by her; the day they met Jerry returned to Nigel and Margaret as if under a spell. He married her in a whirlwind romance before 'she was snapped up by some other lucky fellow' [his words]. Not long afterwards he attended the Staff course at Haifa in Palestine. His brother Nigel was on the same course and recalls that Jerry somehow found time to write to Joy every single day of the course. They were blissfully happy together.

On leaving the Army in 1967, aged fifty-three, Jerry found a job in Horse Racing working for Racehorse Technical Services Ltd. He ran teams that organised the race starts, finishes and race monitoring with remote cameras, travelling the length and breadth of Britain for some ten years.

He was devastated by Joy's death from cancer in 1989 but put a brave face on his circumstances and travelled widely across the globe catching up with many of his old friends. Sadly he then had to cope with a steady deterioration in his diabetes, which became more and more debilitating. In his last few years he found it difficult to get about and gradually restricted himself to a smaller radius close to Malmaison.

He died in Crawley Hospital on 16 February 1998. His ashes are scattered in Malmaison's garden, in the same place as his beloved Joy's were almost ten years earlier.

Jerry aged eighty

8

NIGEL

Major General N H D (Nigel) McGill CB
Born 15 October 1916

Commissioned into the Royal Marines (RM) in 1934. After his young officer training he served briefly in Palestine and joined HMS Repulse off Gibraltar in 1938. Serving on HMS Coventry in the Mediterranean when war broke out, he returned to England with the ship, subsequently undertaking a naval gunnery course and becoming a gunnery instructor. Joined HMS Erebus and sent to reinforce Singapore but Singapore had fallen by the time Erebus had reached Colombo and the ship turned around for Africa, taking part in the capture of Madagascar. Erebus had to dock at Durban in late 1942 for repairs; while there Nigel met Margaret, who later followed him back to England and married him in June 1944. Once repaired, Erebus returned to England in 1943 and Nigel became Adjutant of the RM Officers' Cadet School in Thurlestone, Devon before attending a three-month course with the US Marine Corps at Quantico and then serving with the American Eighth Army in the Philippines in 1945. In 1946 he attended the Staff College at Haifa, at the same time as Jerry. In 1949 he was posted to the Far East with 3 Commando Brigade, after completing the Commando Course, and served in Malaya in the area around Ipoh as a company commander in Batu Gajah with 42 Commando on operations against the communist insurgents, at the same time as Jerry was a staff officer in Kuala Lumpur. He was Mentioned in Despatches in October 1952 for gallant and distinguished service in Malaya, six months after Jerry's similar MID award in April 1952.

After Malaya he commanded the RM Gunnery School at Eastney, Portsmouth, served in the Admiralty with RM Combined Operations, had two years in Washington from 1956–58 as part of the British Defence Staff, ran the RM manning and careers for all the enlisted ranks, and commanded the RM training school at Eastney Barracks, before becoming the Military Secretary in London responsible for the career management of all RM officers. Promoted Major General in 1964, he returned to Eastney Barracks for the third time to run all RM training throughout the UK as MGRM. Awarded CB in 1966 for Command of Portsmouth Group Royal Marines. His final appointment in London in 1967–68 was as the Chief of Staff to the Commandant General Royal Marines. He had three children: Sarah, born 1946; Malcolm, born 1947; Johnny, born 1951.

Nigel's first ship was HMS Repulse which he joined off Gibraltar in 1938 after a brief tour of duty in Palestine. He subsequently joined HMS Coventry in the Mediterranean and returned with Coventry to England shortly after the war started, having fallen seriously ill with jaundice.

HMS Repulse

On manoeuvres in the 1920s, leading other capital ships.

Aerial photograph in the 1920s

Photos from Online Library of US Dept of the Navy, Naval Historical Centre

Back in England, weighing only seven stone, Nigel was nursed back to health in the RN hospital HMS Haslar but was unfit for active service for a further six months so undertook a long gunnery course at HMS Excellent on Whale Island while regaining his strength. He then spent a year instructing RN Sub Lieutenants in naval gunnery before joining HMS Erebus as the gunnery officer and Royal Marine detachment commander. Erebus was a monitor ship built in 1916 in order to bombard the Belgian cost with its two enormous 15 inch guns, capable of firing shells weighing a ton some twenty-five miles with an antiquated fire control system. He took part in two night-time raids on Boulogne harbour, with Erebus sailing from and returning to Chatham under cover of darkness before the Admiralty decided to send the ship to reinforce Singapore.

Fortunately the ship was so slow (top speed 12 knots) that by the time the ship reached Ceylon three months after setting out, via the Azores, Freetown in Sierra Leone, Point Noir in French Equatorial Africa and the Cape, Singapore had fallen. Otherwise it is virtually certain that Erebus would have been sunk by the Japanese. Even so the ship had a narrow escape off Trincomolee when attacked by two formations of Japanese bombers launched from an aircraft carrier. A stick of bombs hit the water only some twenty yards from the starboard side, riddling that side with bomb splinters, killing twenty-two sailors and wounding a further twenty-six. Nigel was on the bridge with the Captain and was knocked over by the blast but otherwise unhurt. The ship was then ordered back to England via Mombasa. While Erebus was at anchor in Mombasa in 1942 Nigel had an unexpected re-union for one day with Dick who had just arrived by troopship from India to take up a staff post in East Africa; the first time the two brothers had seen each other since 1938. En route for the Cape on the return journey, Erebus supported the landing to capture Madagascar in the north-east corner where the French had a small garrison. Later, Nigel managed to take his RM detachment ashore at Majunga for some training.

HMS Erebus in October 1942 off Diego Suarez, Madagascar.
She was built in 1916 to bombard the Belgian Coast in the First World War and
was fitted with two 15 inch guns. Her maximum speed was only 12 knots.

Before reaching the Cape the ship's engines broke down – not surprisingly, as Erebus had been built originally to cross the channel and was not designed for long voyages. The ship had to call at Durban for repairs where Nigel met Margaret and they fell in love after a whirlwind four-month romance.

Margaret and Nigel at Paradise Valley, near Durban, South Africa.

After her repairs HMS Erebus eventually returned to England in 1943, supporting the D-Day landings in Normandy the following year, and Nigel was posted as Adjutant to the Royal Marine Officers Cadet School at Thurlstone in Devon. Back in South Africa it took Margaret a year to find a ship in order to follow Nigel. Eventually she found a berth on the Reinadel Pacificia, a requisitioned troopship in April 1944. Some of her recollections of the voyage, her first arrival in Britain six weeks later, and the nomadic start to her married life with Nigel are described below:

> *There were so many on board that the state rooms were used as dormitories. My friend Audrey Allen and I were in a three-tier bunk on the top level with children, while below us were old missionary nuns, etc. Many of the passengers were refugees from Singapore, who had been waiting for a ship to take them to the UK after its fall to the Japanese. Drinking water was issued, but all*

washing of bodies and clothes was done with seawater, using special seawater soap which left everything sticky. We had to sit on our canvas lifesaving equipment on deck as there were no deckchairs and carry it with us everywhere, as the Jap submarines were in the Indian Ocean. We had innumerable practices in case of a calamity, as we also did later in the Atlantic.

Through the Red Cross we were off loaded into a tented transit camp at Port Tewfik, near Suez, for about four weeks. There we were looked after by Italian prisoners of war but unable to inform anyone of our whereabouts. The camp was called 'The Aviary'. Audrey was with me, as were other service wives and children, disabled army and navy personnel and the missionary nuns. Audrey and I shared our tent with another woman and her two children. Washing was primitive and food hardly adequate, but we found a NAAFI close by which helped. We made friends with the odd units we met in the NAAFI from the surrounding American, South African and British military camps, who invited us to their various canteens for a proper meal. We visited the Americans for their food and ice cream and the South Africans for their fruit; but not the British because their rations were so dreary.

There was a huge high wire fence around our Aviary, but Audrey and I persuaded the corporal on duty to allow us to creep back in through a hole he had made should we be later than 10 p.m. The Pioneer Corps took us on a ride to Cairo in a jeep where we visited the Souk and the Sphinx and, although Suez was out of bounds due to bubonic plague, the jeep took us to swim in the canal at the French Club in Ismailia.

We resumed voyage in a hospital ship, the Alcantara, on its way to the UK from India, and eventually docked in Glasgow on 30 May. Very excited, I rang Nigel, with Audrey holding me up in the phone booth, but, sounding

*very remote, all he could manage was 'Oh, that's good'!
He later explained his apparent reticence was due to all
the Wrens listening in at his elbow. Audrey and I hauled
our trunks on to a train (no porters) and sat up all night
on them in the crowded train to London.*

*Arriving in London on 31 May, we found there was
no one to meet us so we taxied to South Africa House
in Trafalgar Square only to find it shut because it was
the South African National Day. So we sat on the bot-
tom step and wept – before pulling ourselves together
and continuing our journey to Ockley in Surrey where
Gladys Bosworth lived, an aunt-by-marriage, to see if
she could put us up until we could find somewhere to
live. Britain was preparing for D-Day and was beset
with doodlebugs (V-1 rockets), blackouts, food rationing, clothing coupons, restricted travel, and virtually no
petrol. Nigel had no home in the UK as his parents had
been caught in Jersey when the Germans overran the
Channel Islands.*

*Nigel managed to see me in Ockley, arriving by bi-
cycle, before being whisked off on D-Day itself (6 June)
to Inverary for an amphibious warfare course. Gladys
promptly had a heart attack, so Jack and Sheila Carter
(friends of Nigel nearby in Dorking) kindly put me up
and even arranged the whole wedding in St Martin's
Church in Dorking on 24th June when Nigel returned.
I had no expectation of having a proper wedding gown
as it was wartime and I only had one friend in the UK
(Audrey). The Carters suggested my wearing Sheila's
altered blue wedding dress and shoes and I found a veil
(on coupons) locally. I had brought a fruit cake soldered
into a tin and drowned in brandy, plus extra sugar, fats
and raisins in my luggage from Durban. The Carters,
who were of great help throughout, arranged tea, etc.,
for a small reception in their house. There were only
a few Royal Marine couples living locally, including*

Nigel's best man Skarn Akham (second choice – the other had gone to sea!). Nigel had to have a special licence from the Vicar General in Westminster Abbey to be married so quickly because he was soon to leave for Quantico in the USA.

The wedding party occupied only two pews in that huge church. Jack Carter gave me away and Audrey came as my bridesmaid, in her pink velvet evening dress she'd brought over (a bit hot for June!). The Carters made sandwiches and a cake or two for a small reception on their terrace. Afterwards we were taken to the station to go by train to the Birch Hotel in Haywards Heath for a few days. Later we were lent a cottage in Linchmere, near Haslemere, for a week. We had two miles to walk to Liphook, and two miles back carrying provisions – no car, no bicycles, no buses, with doodlebugs dropping now and then. From the cottage we moved to the Cumberland in Marble Arch but this was too expensive, so while Nigel was at the RM office, I bussed around London looking for accommodation, very lost and bewildered. We landed up in Frognal, Finchley Road, in a small hotel, where Nigel heard that his brother Malcolm had been killed in Burma the previous month. Nigel then sailed for Quantico, USA on 25 July.

I found a job in the canteen (hours, 8 a.m.–3 p.m. or 3–10 p.m.) at the Springbok Club in Princes Gate, an off-shoot of the South African Embassy, which took pity on me. Until Nigel returned, I moved myself to a B&B in Queens Gate (£3 per week, including meals) because travelling from Frognal during doodlebug scares was no joke. However, I only had to lie in the gutter once, behind the Albert Hall, because of a bomb. The canteen was quite amusing because many South Africans passed through, either on leave or en route somewhere. Old boyfriends emerged now and then, and so out to dinner and dancing sometimes. There was one irate major who created a scene because his porridge had already been sugared in the kitchen (due to rationing), and being a South African, he especially liked his sugar. I had no washing up and no cooking, so it wasn't a chore being there.

At Queens Gate, we spent some time in the cubby-hole under the staircase when doodlebugs were over, mainly to escape the flying glass. I managed to buy one mealie (corn cob) and boiled it in a kettle in my room one evening feeling homesick with no Nigel there.

Nigel returned after four months and we celebrated with a day or two in the Cadogan Hotel. Later, we found a top-floor flat in Notting Hill Gate with the sink at the top of the stairs. We had the next seven weeks together for a change before Nigel was off again, this time to the Philippines until mid-April 1945.

After the war Nigel returned to Palestine, this time as a student on the staff course at Haifa. He then had a variety of short assignments before moving to a posting in London for two years, living in Reigate with Margaret and their first two children, Sarah and Malcolm.

Quantico in 1944.

Haifa in 1946

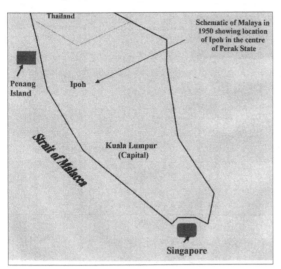

In 1950 Nigel was commanding B Company, 42 Commando in Hong Kong when the Commando, together with 3 Commando Brigade, was sent to Malaya where British Forces were engaged in a guerrilla war against communist terrorists from the Malayan Races Liberation Army (MRLA) led by Chin Peng and supported mainly by ethnic Chinese living in Malaya. MRLA guerrillas had killed three British rubber planters in Serak in June 1948, which resulted in a state of emergency being declared.

The British and Malayan security forces eventually defeated the terrorists by a combination of denying them access to food and shelter by resettling people living in jungle areas to fortified villages; good intelligence; effective partnership between the Police and the Army; aggressive patrolling to disrupt the terrorists; and an effective 'hearts and minds' campaign. Overall a total of some forty thousand British and Commonwealth troops were deployed against an estimated peak of seven to eight thousand communist terrorists. Once Malaya became independent in 1957 the insurrection lost its rationale as a war of liberation against colonial masters and the resistance petered out in 1958 with remaining MRLA terrorists moving to the Thai border and further north. The Malayan government declared the Emergency was over in 1960 and Chin Peng fled to China. During the conflict, 519 British military and 1,346 Malayan troops were killed; 2,478 civilians were killed with an additional 810 recorded as missing. The MRLA lost 6,710 killed and 1,287 captured plus some 3,000 who surrendered. (Figures taken from Wikipedia.)

Brigade Headquarters and 42 Commando Headquarters were in Ipoh (in the state of Perak) and Nigel's company were in Batu Gajah some twenty miles away, responsible for an area the size of a small county in England.

Nigel and Margaret, Jerry, Dick in 1955 outside Briar Cottage.
Dick's first visit to England since before the war and
the first reunion of the surviving brothers since 1938.

Nigel based his company in the location of the Government Rest House and worked closely with the district commissioner, chief of police and local businessmen, farmers and miners. There were a number of alluvial tin mines in the state. Insurgent activity was initially high with the terrorists hiding in the jungle in the mountain range that ran past Ipoh down to Batu Gajah and coming out frequently to terrorise the local population. Soon after arriving and the day after Nigel had driven through the village of Poo Sing, the terrorists clubbed the village head teacher and chief of police to death in front of the school children. Nigel instigated an active programme of patrols that did not follow any set pattern or routine; the company soon reduced the number of terrorist incidents and killed a bandit within a month. The company made extensive use of their two attached Eban trackers (father and son) who got on well with the marines. They did suffer one reverse while Nigel was leading a patrol on the trail of some bandits in thick

111

jungle, when they were ambushed by the terrorists they were chasing. In the sudden crash of gunfire a marine was shot in the shoulder and a young English police lieutenant immediately behind Nigel was badly wounded in the groin. The terrorists vanished and evaded the patrol's follow-up drills. The remaining members of the patrol carried the policeman back out of the jungle for an exhausting four hours on a makeshift stretcher of bamboo poles and rifle slings. They then drove him to the local European hospital but he died that night.

Nigel remained in Malaya for two and a half years; first as a company commander, followed by a stint at Headquarters 42 Commando where he coordinated all the administrative and logistic support for the unit, and finally as the DAA and QMG of 3 Commando Brigade for over a year. As well as 42 Commando, the Brigade included a Gurkha battalion plus another British infantry battalion, a light armoured regiment and a sapper squadron. He enjoyed the experience and greatly respected his two Brigade Commanders, Campbell Hardie and Cecil Phillips. The intrepid Margaret joined him in Ipoh with Sarah and Malcolm; Johnny, the youngest, was born in the hospital in Batu Gajah in 1951.

On leaving Malaya, the family moved for a short period to Malta before returning to the UK in September 1952. In 1953, Nigel wisely bought their first house, Briar Cottage in Ascot, which they kept until he left the Royal Marines fifteen years later.

On retiring from the Royal Marines Nigel worked for Rolls Royce for nine years where he implemented a career planning and management system for senior managers. He and Margaret bought a house in Atlow, near Ashbourne in Derbyshire. After his second retirement in 1977 they finally settled in Fordingbridge near the New Forest in their home Alderwood. They have always welcomed family and friends and they generously provided me with a wonderful home in Eastney and Derbyshire for five years when I first came to England and before I married Mary.

Nigel – three months before his ninetieth birthday.

Nigel's medals.
CB, Royal Naval GSM with MID Oak Leaf and 3 bars of service in Malaya
plus Palestine before and after the war 1939–45 Star, Atlantic Star, Burma Star,
Defence Medal, 1939–45 War Medal, Coronation Medal, Jubilee Medal

9

RHODESIA

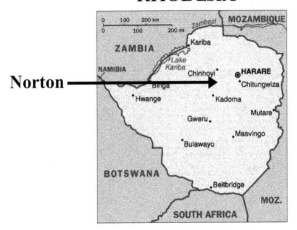

Norton →

*Map from the Univesity of Texas Online Collection – www.lib.utexas.edu/maps
Courtesy of the University of Texas Libraries, the University of Texas at Austin*

*Map of Zimbabwe (previously known as Rhodesia). Harare was Salisbury.
Norton (location of Dick's farm) is twenty-five miles SW of Harare.*

SS Tairea reached Beira in Mozambique in December 1947, having first called at Mombasa. Dick and his family, including Frances' parents, travelled on to Rhodesia by train. Sadly my grandmother Blanche, Frances' mother, fell seriously ill on the last stage of the journey and died in hospital on 26 December 1947, within a few days of arriving in Salisbury, having found the journey from India too much for her. A little more than eighteen months later my grandfather Cecil, Frances' father, died on 1 August 1949 aged eighty-six.

A major reason for moving to Rhodesia was due to one of my mother's uncles, Commander Teddy Tyndale-Biscoe RN, who, as a young man, had joined Cecil Rhodes' pioneer column with responsibility for the guns and searchlights and had raised the Union Jack at Fort Salisbury soon after the pioneers' arrival. After some years' gold digging and fighting in both the Matabele and Mashona wars, he had returned to England with wonderful stories about the country, which enticed not only my parents but other Tyndale-Biscoe cousins to settle in this developing country. Additionally, my father had served with Major Richard Fleming from Rhodesia and a Black Watch officer (in the same headquarters in Nairobi during the War) who had warmly encouraged him to move there and who subsequently became one of Dick's greatest friends.

Dick, Richard (at back) and Ian outside Dunedin
(the family's first house in Salisbury) in 1949.

My parents, Richard and I moved into a rented house in Salisbury while Dick supervised the building of a new house on the outskirts of the town and found work with the National Mutual Life Assurance Society as an insurance representative. He much enjoyed travelling around the country and meeting people but he was not a natural salesman and could not help himself pointing out the snags (as well as the benefits) of the policies he was trying to sell! He especially admired the farmers' fortitude, resilience and humour and it was not long before he decided to try his luck farming. In April 1950 the family (which now included Julia, born eighteen months earlier) moved to Norton, to Four Winds Farm where my father worked as a farm assistant for a short time to learn about farming. At the same time he bought a four hundred-acre plot nearby which he called 'Swallowfield' and moved the family into a very basic new home there in time for the New Year.

He kept in close touch with his mother and surviving two brothers and was always interested in their news, especially while Jerry and Nigel were both in Malaya on operations, but nearly all his energy was now focused on farming. Just before moving to Swallowfield he wrote to Jerry.

Four Winds Farm, PO Norton, S Rhodesia
12 November 1950

My dear old Jerry,

I am writing this in plenty of time to reach you for Xmas. It brings you & Joy our very best wishes for success & happiness for the coming year. We will think of you in far off Malaya and hope that someday we may have the opportunity of having a family reunion. You must think that you have been more or less forgotten, but not a bit of it. You are often in our thoughts.

You would smile if you saw how we lived; talk about a squash – we have the children on top of us day & night! We hope to be on our farm 'Swallowfield' by the New Year & though the cottage we are building is pretty minute, it is more conveniently designed than this shack on Mortimer's farm.

The world news is very disturbing: what with Korea now turning really ugly with the Chinese forces joining in; Indo China; Malaya; Tibet and now this revolution in Nepal. It would seem that Russia is fighting very successfully by proxy. S Rhodesia has raised a small volunteer force for service in Malaya; it will be on its way very soon. I also understand that a number of ex-Gurkha Brigade officers have been offered attractive terms of service to return to the Brigade in Malaya. Is this a fact? I gather they are very short of officers.

One hears very little of what is happening in Malaya. I suppose the new measures are having effect. I dare say Margaret and family will have arrived in Penang by now. It's a great pity that Nigel cannot have them with him. Mother seems to think that Nigel has left his unit and gone to some staff appointment. I didn't gather this at all – can you enlighten me?

We plod along in our farming operations. The rains have come & if all goes well we will be planting on our first lands this week. All very exciting really! I have three eight-acre tobacco lands & two eight-acre lands for velvet beans & monkey nuts. Most of the buildings are more or less complete.

God Bless & all the v best, Dick.

Meanwhile, my grandmother Emily had travelled to Rhodesia to catch up with Dick, whom she'd not seen since before the war, and to meet her daughter-in-law (Frances) and the three grandchildren for the first time. She planned at first just to come for a three-month visit before then continuing to Malaya to see Jerry and Nigel. Now aged seventy-three she initially appeared to thrive on the change and in a letter to Jerry a year after her arrival it even seemed that she would settle in Salisbury:

'The Corner House', Devon Road, Avondale West,
Salisbury, S Rhodesia
10 April 1951

My very dearest Jerry,

It gave me such pleasure to receive your letter; some little time past. I had begun to think you had forgotten my existence. I am glad to hear that Nigel and you see something of each other now and again. I wish I also had that pleasure. Well, here am I at long last settled in a nice little house of my own. The constant moving about was not always convenient, as it is terribly difficult to hear of accommodation in or near Salisbury. The lady I was living with in Livingstone Avenue had several heart attacks & suddenly decided to leave her house & go to the Cape. No hotel will take you in for more than five nights at a time, so I suddenly made up my mind to buy a house if a suitable one was available and be independent on my own once more. I went to five agents and the last one took me to see five houses. This was the last I saw and I decided at once to buy it and all was settled and paid within three hours.

I wish you & Joy could come & visit me here. I am busy making a garden & already have vegetables & flowers & am planting some flowering trees & shrubs. The neighbours are pleasant & kind. A man from Jersey is in the next house & he called on me to ask if he could help me in any way. There is a good bus service to Salisbury, fifteen minutes' drive from here.

Dick & Frances have been to see me several times & soon I'm going to visit them in their new farm house, which Dick has built himself, helped by native labour. Dick has even done all the plumbing work. He is a most capable man & seems to be able to turn his hand to anything. The rains have been very poor this season so the crops are not very good, which is a great disappointment to all farmers. I have never seen Dick & Frances look so well & they are very happy. The children are splendid. Richard is soon home again from his school in Bulawayo; he comes by plane. Little Julia is killingly amusing, & is such a neat, dainty little person, with a charming manner & smile. Ian is busy all day, riding his donkey on the farm & telling his father what is the best sort of manure to use!

I had a letter from Margaret in which she mentions

Sarah & Malcolm [Margaret, Sarah & Malcolm had now recently joined Nigel in Malaya] had whooping cough, but now much better, & the other day a letter from Nigel which stated that the children are OK again. It is a nasty thing but nowadays they give injections which help very much.

The temperatures remain fairly high still though our summer is now over & soon winter will start. Most days it is 80° to 85° in the shade but it is very lovely with a nice cool breeze; practically no mosquitoes & few flies. At present I am busy furnishing & making curtains. The shops are good in Salisbury but rather more expensive than in Capetown [she'd travelled from Britain via Capetown]. I do most of the cooking myself. The fruit here is lovely; I have grapes, mangos, oranges, bananas being sold by natives who come to the house regularly. Beef here is poor so I am practically a vegetarian, which is a good thing in this climate. I get good milk & as much as I want and the Avondale Stores call daily for all groceries which is most convenient – & the baker also calls daily.

Must stop now & go to bed. It is 9.30 p.m. & I'm always up at 6 a.m. Do write again, dear, before long & let us keep in touch.

Much love to Joy & you & hoping all is well.

Your affectionate Mother.

Sadly, Emily never really settled in Rhodesia and returned to England in 1953 after some three years trying to adapt to a very different lifestyle, compared to her upbringing in Scotland and her home in Jersey before the war. Within a year she died in England.

Life as a new farmer was very challenging, especially as my father had to borrow money in order to develop the farm (buildings, machinery, etc.) and to pay for each year's outlay on new crops (seeds, fertilizer, wages, etc.). On a good year the profits from the crop would pay off the annual loan from the Rhodesian Land Bank and Dick would invest the remainder into the farm. For the first couple of years the lifestyle was pretty primitive; no running water or power, the loo being a grass shack sheltering a wooden seat over a deep hole in the ground, bath water heated in a forty-gallon drum over a fire and carried by hand into the bathroom (and subsequently emptied by hand), lighting provided by paraffin lamps and the water provided from a well. Two of the first essentials were a borehole and generator. In addition to growing tobacco, Dick worked long hours to organise a safe electrical supply powered from the generator until mains power was available some years later (from the power lines running from the Kariba Dam) and to sort out a water storage tank and the pipes and plumbing for the house and the garden. An extract from a letter written by my father to Jerry in August 1951 provides a brief insight:

> *Farming operations and more building are occupying all my time. Two more barns (each 25,000 bricks – made on the farm), a grading shed, a reservoir (25,000 gallons), together with several miscellaneous buildings will occupy all my time and take all my money. The new tobacco season starts on 1 September when we sow our seedbeds. This is a tricky operation and has to be very carefully done. Good seedbeds are the basis of one's crop. I am putting in 50 acres this year of tobacco, 10 acres maize, 10 acres velvet beans & 10 acres of monkey nuts. In addition we have 2 acres of orchard, one acre of lucerne, one acre of vegetables, 3 acres of mealies & 10 acres of blue gums plantation. Besides this, Fluffy is busy with her chickens & turkeys (we have 70 turkeys and about 150 hens).*
>
> *We have no tractor on the farm. All our field work is done by oxen of which I have one and a half spans; i.e. twenty-four in all. This is a slow process as we can only plough three acres a day, whereas a tractor can finish eight or nine. Nor have we a lorry. Our only form*

of transport is a Ford 3/4-ton vanette & a 3-ton trailer which six oxen pull. Last year I had a one-ton jeep truck four-wheel drive which did us excellently as it pulled the trailer as well, but it was heavy on petrol and uncomfortable for the family. I sold it three months ago and got a 1951 Ford Vanette, which is a nice job. To capitalise a farm is a tremendous undertaking in these expensive times. Buildings alone cost the earth, whilst one's labour takes a big chunk. We couldn't survive another season like this one. Because of the drought the leaf has no body at all and only a small percentage has much colour. Many a tobacco farmer has been ruined. It's always a gamble but a reasonable one.

Over time, Dick built Swallowfield into a successful farm and very friendly family home. He later managed to buy another 400-acre plot, which he called Thornbury, some eight miles away for growing maize (with a richer soil – reddish in colour – compared to the more sandy-coloured soil at Swallowfield) and gradually switched from growing tobacco to concentrating on growing maize (some 200–250 acres each year) and raising around a hundred head of beef cattle. In addition we always had a few cows for our milk, around two hundred chickens which provided eggs for sale, a few ducks and a couple of geese, horses, dogs and cats. It was an idyllic lifestyle for the family but Dick was always working extremely hard. In order to make ends meet he used to take an extra job for about three months each winter as the local agent for the Grain Marketing Board, responsible for loading and despatching all the maize grown in the Norton area (destined for the Grain Marketing Board) at the local railway station.

Life on a farm anywhere is full of surprises and uncertainty; Swallowfield was no exception and provided some unique experiences for Dick and all the family. In the early years the roofs of two or three of the tobacco barns were blown off twice by tremendous storms that also dumped over seven inches of rain overnight – right in the middle of the curing season. We were rescued by the generous help from our neighbour Eric Varley, who kindly made a couple of his barns available until the roofs were repaired, even though this inevitably affected his own reaping schedule. The farmhouse was built very close to a large anthill, which also provided an ideal spot for snake holes. When it rained, the snakes very often slithered into the house for a bit of shelter; over the first few years, my father killed many snakes either in the house or in the garden – some extremely venomous ones, including puff adders, boomslangs, mambas and cobras – aided by our cats, which were very effective hunters. Sadly there were, no doubt, some harmless grass snakes despatched. There was always great excitement and a hullabaloo among the African labourers when a snake was spotted. I well remember being asked to 'come quickly', because there was a 'nyoka fanana football jersey' that turned out to be a banded cobra close to the stables! Fortunately, the horses were in the paddock.

My father had a natural affinity for people of all types and all races and was well respected by his farm workers; not so my mother, who struggled with the local African language and who was very often ignored by the farm Africans. Dick preferred to employ Africans from Malawi (then Nyasaland) as they were generally happier working on a farm than the local Shona tribesmen, and he had taken the trouble to learn Chinyanja (the Nyasaland native language), so had a good rapport with them. In many ways it was a paternal existence with my father providing his workers with everything in return for their labour. They in turn demonstrated an unusual loyalty and the core team he started with at Swallowfield remained with him for twenty years – as did some of their children.

He provided each farm worker with a small plot of land on which he could build his house (or a collection of houses, according to how many wives he had), keep some chickens and grow some mealies. He fed them their rations every week; meat, mealie-meal, salt, sugar, beans and monkey nuts (those with families received more than the single men). He provided the means for them to brew their local beer – normally entrusted to the longer-serving workers who would take it in turns to concoct the brew which they would then sell to the labour force in a weekly party starting every Saturday afternoon and ending once all the beer was drunk, often not until the next morning. The success of the party was normally judged by the size of the hangovers and the redness of the eyes amongst those turning up for work on the Monday morning! He ran sick parades and treated the minor ailments such as cuts, upset or blocked-up stomachs, headaches, etc. as best he could. He ferried the labourers (and their wives or children) to the nearest doctor or local African clinic in his car – often in the middle of the night. He paid his workers every month in cash, which he collected from the bank and kept in the farm safe until payday. He built and funded a school for their children, including paying the teacher's salary, and my mother ran a local store on the farm that stocked basic groceries, clothing and hardware items which the local Africans bought and which also supplemented the family income.

Often one or more of the farm workers would ask for credit, usually for something like a bicycle, or to pay for one of their elder children to attend a senior school, or in order to pay the bride price for a wife. There was a particularly quiet and gentle man, called Douglas, who was often beaten up by his wife, usually during a beer-drinking weekend. One day she went too far and almost severed his foot with a badza (an implement used for cultivating her patch of mealies), so Douglas kicked her out of his home and offered her to the highest bidder. Mrs Douglas was reckoned to be a pretty good cook and a month or two later one of the workers called Chingasama approached my father for some credit. When Dick enquired what for, he rather shyly said he had decided to take Mrs Douglas on as his wife and needed the money to pay Douglas. When my father then asked how much he wanted, he replied, 'Twelve pounds.'

'Twelve pounds!' my father exclaimed. 'For Mrs Douglas! Do you know that you can buy a brand new bicycle for that?'

Whereupon Chingasama thought for a while and then said, 'OK, twelve pounds is much too expensive; just give me two pounds, please!!'

Dick was heartened by his farm workers' sense of humour but sometimes exasperated by their lack of responsibility. When he could eventually afford to pay for a tractor, his tractor drivers would sometimes continue ploughing, despite symptoms of the engine overheating, until the engine would seize. They were always reluctant to check the oil or water, as they did not consider simple maintenance to be part of their 'driver's job'. Hence Dick would have to supervise every morning, ensuring that they personally carried out a 'First Parade' maintenance check of the tractors. He also personally had to check the temperature and humidity of every tobacco barn every few hours by night during the curing season, as the man he put in charge of the barns at night would often fall asleep.

By the early 1960s the pressure for political change in the Federation of Rhodesia and Nyasaland was inexorably growing. Northern Rhodesia and Nyasaland would soon become independent of Britain, self-governing, and changed their names to Zambia and Malawi. The future for Southern Rhodesia, developing fast and with a thriving economy, was subject to pressures both internally and externally; not only the UK but also America and the UN would influence its future. Dick understood this but he was becoming concerned that the politicians within the Federation and further afield did not really understand the issues. Furthermore, he had very little respect for them!

Extract from a letter to Jerry on 19 March 1962

The political set-up here is bewildering. The only person who wants the Federation to continue is Welensky [then Prime Minister of the Federation] & he seems to be losing his grip recently. We here in S Rhodesia would like to go it alone as Whitehead [then Prime Minister of Southern Rhodesia – defeated in the 1962 election by the Rhodesian Front] has so often said. The politicians, the avaricious ones, however, have their eyes on the N Rhodesian copper mines which each year account for a significant part of the Federation's total revenue. We in S Rhodesia would have to tighten our belts, but our economy is not at all unbalanced, being agricultural, mining and industrial. No one minds the black man getting into power but heaven protect us from the black extremist who is almost fanatical in his dislike of the whites. Anyway, the fact that Rab Butler [then British Deputy PM] has been appointed Minister for Central Africa seems rather significant. We are dining with the Alports' tomorrow [Cub Alport was the British High Commissioner to the Federation] so hope to get the low-down from him. Thank heavens I'm not actively involved in politics. Those of my friends who were really decent people before they went into Parliament are so busy double-crossing themselves and their constituents that they have become split personalities. What a dirty game it is. The British Government hasn't shown up too well either. The main point is that no moderate-thinking white has any objection to eventually allowing the African to become independent, but as things are at present the Black Nationalist extremist invariably resorts to intimidation to gain his way. The 'one man one vote' cry is absurd at this stage when 75% of the electorate can so easily be swayed by threats. Believe me when I say that they [the African population] are frightened far worse than we are.

Extract from a letter in November 1962 to Jerry and Joy (from Frances) after some unrest in Southern Rhodesia and a call-out of Reserve Policemen

Life here goes on as usual – on the surface anyway. The only effect the 'Emergency' had on us was that Dick was called out in his capacity as a Reserve Policeman for a week on eight-hour shifts every twenty-four hours. His job was the Control Officer on the wireless sets at Police HQ in Norton; taking messages from Area HQ in Salisbury concerning reported incidents which he relayed to the eight local patrols of Reserve Police working in jeeps, each with their own sets, and to the helicopter and armoured cars (manned by Territorials) which were also covering our area (nine hundred sq. miles). This enables arson, stoning, intimidation, theft, etc. to be dealt with in double quick time. Luckily there were only a few fires on farm lands and one stolen car here. Our Police Reservists in Norton are nearly all local farmers so they managed to have a good 'get-together' during the course of their patrols. In S Rhodesia the Police Reserves and Special Constables (who patrol the towns) number 28,000 (including 7,500 Africans) so you can see that everyone is determined things won't get out of hand here as they did in Kenya.

Meanwhile while the flap was on, I minded the farm, well guarded by our four dogs. Our workforce (thirty-two Africans) weren't interested in the unrest and carried on as normal. Luckily Ian was home for the school holidays and having just got his driving licence (at sixteen here) helped a lot, driving the truck and tractors and helping with supervision, though Dick of course had to carry straight on with farm work when he came off his night shifts which was pretty exhausting.

Scenes from Swallowfield

Ploughing a field using oxen

Regular dipping of oxen was essential to kill any ticks they carried. The oxen were made to swim through a tank filled with a mixture of water and insecticide

Frances and Julia in a tobacco field, shortly before it was ready for reaping (harvesting)

Reaping the tobacco was the busiest time of the year. Everyone on the farm, including the wives, helped

127

A team of oxen hauling recently reaped tobacco

*Dick towing a trailer with some of the farm workers and reaped tobacco.
Ian and Julia are sitting behind Dick*

*The start of the first
two tobacco barns.
The bricks for all the
buildings were made
on the farm*

Putting the roof on the grading shed. A tobacco barn is in the background

Dick with Ian and Julia in 1952 at Swallowfield

The farm house in 1955 – four years after moving to Swallowfield

Dick made time to play cricket with Ian whenever possible during the school holidays. Julia is more interested in the cat! The farm cottage is in the background

Dick and Frances with (from left):
Julia, Richard and Ian – 1963

Dick & Julia with a hungry cow

Winston and Jo (two faithful companions)

Maize Fields on Thornbury, some eight miles from Swallowfield

A typical maize field varied from fifty to a hundred+ acres

View of a maize field just before welcome rain

Dick and Ian

Although bush pigs and baboons sometimes caused significant damage to the maize crop, the most serious threat was drought. The rains were always welcomed.

Maize was less risky and involved less work than tobacco, although it was not generally as profitable. It was a relief for Dick to get out of tobacco once the link with cancer became irrefutable – and he certainly did not miss the chore of checking on the tobacco barns three times a night during the reaping and curing season which lasted some three months each year.

On top of his farming and family responsibilities, Dick became Chairman of Hopelands Trust for Mentally Handicapped children and adults, and played a major role in setting it up, together with Frances, who acted as Secretary. My elder brother, Richard, was born handicapped, due to a very difficult and protracted birth with resultant oxygen starvation. There was nowhere suitable for him in Rhodesia and it took Dick and Frances some time to accept that Richard was really struggling. He attended normal schools until he was eleven years old – boarding first at a prep school in Bulawayo three hundred miles from Norton and then attending the local Norton school. They then found a place for Richard in a Rudolf Steiner home in England and later at Hermanus near Capetown, but were determined to provide a better future for mentally handicapped children in Rhodesia.

By 1957 a group of parents (together with Dick and Frances) had formed a committee and set about solving the problem. They named their organisation Hopelands, electing Dick as Chairman and, in 1959, a generous couple donated a place intended as a holiday home for children in Umvukwes to Hopelands, which first started with about ten boys. Soon afterwards another location in Salisbury was offered by the Mashonaland Diocese and, later, two further homes were set up in Bulawayo and near Salisbury. At the time of his death, Dick had been Chairman for nearly fourteen years and the Hopelands Trust was then looking after just over three hundred mentally handicapped boys, girls and adults at the four separate locations. Richard by then had joined a Hopelands home at a place called Homefield, not far from Salisbury. Dick and Frances dedicated much of their lives to mentally handicapped people, but the struggle surely took its toll on Dick's reserves.

Frances describing her and Dick's work for Hopelands Trust in a letter in November 1962 to Jerry and Joy...

Hopelands still takes up all our spare time as Dick took over the Chair again in Feb. There are now eighty-one children, young men and girls, of whom twenty come daily to the two schools, one training centre and one community centre. Trying to get financial support from the Government is our chief headache. At this criti-

cal juncture there isn't the money to spare for Social Services as in the UK. Our costs are now £30,000 pa and there's a limit to what voluntary contributors can do. Some of the parents pay fees but only about 25% can afford the full fees of £300 pa and some pay nothing.

The other headache is finding staff as people trained in this work don't exist in this country. However, we do have a few very fine people who have become terribly keen and the results they achieve in many cases are amazing. We must just trust that more like them will come forward.

The young children, many of whom can do nothing for themselves when they come to Hopelands and have to be taught even to play, are given special remedial education by trained teachers who have to learn the special methods. A few learn to read and write and the majority who can't absorb the three Rs are taught handwork. All are trained in social behaviour and learn to make beds, lay the tables, wash up and so on. They are encouraged in social contacts by being taken for outings, picnics, concerts, and so on and visitors are encouraged to join in with them at social events and film shows, etc., at school.

The bigger boys go on to a training centre where they learn farm work, gardening, how to look after cows, pigs and poultry – and to do brick making, plastering and simple building, house painting, etc. Those that are unsuited to outside work learn simple carpentry, rug making, weaving, baking and cooking. One boy supplies all the bread and rolls for the Centre and many surrounding households. They also undertake easy light industrial work such as making wire coat hangers, lamp shades, rubber door mats, etc. The local people rally round and provide the social contact needed.

The older girls stay on at the schools and help look after the little ones, do the housework and laundry and *are taught sewing, embroidery, doll making and dressing, etc. They made £100 by selling what they'd made at a fete last year and a further £40 recently.*

When they are grown up the young men and women, who have matured sufficiently in their personalities, move on to the village community centre which has just been opened on a 120-acre farm let. This is run at present by an ex-farmer and his wife who's a nurse and who will be joined by another couple shortly. The young men run the farm and/or carry on with their carpentry and light sheltered industry. The girls look after the houses and spend part of their time in their 'doll' factory and sewing room. They all, too, enjoy social contact with the friends of Hopelands who join in the evening activities. In time, we hope that this community centre will become self-supporting and that the young people can earn a small wage from what they sell. At present there are twelve young men and women there. Later the numbers will grow to sixty and then it will be necessary to establish another such centre.

Dr Weihs, Superintendent of the Rudolf Steiner Camphill Schools, who was Hopeland's inspiration when it was formed in 1957, came out on a visit in June and told us that a good beginning had been made and that Hopelands was on the right lines, which was very cheering for us all. His actual words to the Press were 'When one considers that this work in Britain enjoys strong Government support, the true value of the Hopelands contribution can be seen'. Anyway we find it all most absorbing and only wish we could devote all our time to it.

In November 1965, Ian Smith, then Prime Minister of Rhodesia, declared UDI (the Unilateral Declaration of Independence). I had just started at Sandhurst and had been enlisted into the British Army, Julia was still at school in Salisbury and Richard had recently settled at Homefield. My father was naturally worried about the eventual outcome in Rhodesia and believed that its long-term future needed the majority of the population (the Africans) having a say in their future.

The day after UDI, Dick started pulling up half of his tobacco crop, recently transplanted from the seedbeds, as he knew that the market would suffer due to adverse world opinion, especially British, about Rhodesian politics – and he did not want to waste his scarce resources in cultivating the whole crop for little or even a negative return. A neighbouring farmer (who was subsequently murdered on his farm during the later terrorist war) called on Dick to enquire why he had pulled out so much of his crop. Dick invited him in for a beer and explained why, whereupon his neighbour exclaimed: 'Jeez, man, that's a bloody stupid thing you're doing – us whites have got to stick up for the country and show who's in charge.' My father replied that it wasn't a case of patriotism but one of realism and that there was no point in wasting money cultivating a crop that was unlikely to have a market. The neighbour then told Dick that his beer 'was sticking in his throat and he was going to throw it out of the window' – which he promptly did and drove away. Not everyone acted the same as this particular neighbour, but Ian Smith and his Rhodesian Front Party struck a chord with many Rhodesian whites, especially those who had not lived in other countries and who could not imagine other non-white races having ability and talent. The following year, when I was back on leave from Sandhurst and playing cricket for Norton one Sunday, the same individual told me that he considered me 'a bloody traitor and that he would make sure he shot me should the British ever dare to invade Rhodesia'. Fortunately the other team members (also local farmers) told him not to be so stupid and reassured me that I was welcome in the team! The point about these two stories is that they reflected a tension in Rhodesia that saddened my father enormously. He retained a deep loyalty for the British Crown and he was disappointed that his links with his mother country would inevitably become strained. Additionally, he could not help foreseeing that Rhodesia, previously so full of promise, was bound to struggle and that the days of a peaceful partnership between the whites and blacks were over. Nevertheless, he had a great affection for the country and admired the endeavour of the white settlers, particularly the farmers, who had done so much to develop it. Some of his anxiety, confusion and frustration is illustrated in excerpts from four letters around this time to Jerry:

Letter 31 October 1965 (11 days before UDI)

You have doubtless been reading all about the Independence issue in the Press. Rhodesia appears to have been World news for some considerable time. Frances & I & thousands of sensible people are against UDI but at the same time we are also very much against majority rule. Let us hope that his latest idea of a Royal Commission appointed to see whether Independence can possibly be granted in the 1961 Constitution could work the miracle so necessary to break the deadlock. UDI would spell economic disaster. It's a crazy set-up altogether.

Of course when we read & hear what is going on in Kenya, the Congo, Tanzania, Zambia, Ghana & Nigeria one can't blame the average white Rhodesian for trying to take steps to avoid a similar state of affairs coming about here. All those countries except Zambia (which has copper) are politically independent but economically dependent on outside aid. We on the other hand get no 'million dollar hand-outs' & never have. Economically we are very viable & given negotiated independence this country could go ahead v fast. And in the 1961 Constitution the black man will have the majority vote within ten to fifteen years. I cannot see why the whole world gets so hot under the collar. After all, America declared UDI after the 1773 Boston Tea Party. The only difference being that She liquidated most of the Red Indians. Yet since 1948 the African population here has increased from 2.75 million to 4 million. The whole Western World has been taken for a ride by our Yankee allies.

Do so hope you enjoyed your Italian trip. Was the weather kind to you? I expect you found difficulty in recognising the old familiar landmarks. I see that the monastery at Cassino has been completely rebuilt. One of these days I would like to take Frances on the battlefields from Rimini to the Po and show her where the Battalion [2nd/8th Gurkha Rifles] fought.

Letter 4 December 1965

Many people here of the same persuasion as ourselves who don't approve of UDI and the way it was taken are becoming more and more disgusted at Wilson's antics. In the end I feel we may be forced into the Smith camp, because at least he is governing decently & law & order are being maintained. By imposing the severest of economic sanctions Britain is punishing Rhodesia. But by freezing all personal bank accounts she is hitting those people with British passports who are what we may term the Loyalists; i.e. the Queen's men as opposed to what Wilson refers to the 'Rebels' i.e. Smith's men. My account at Lloyds is frozen & I cannot send a penny from here. One gets the impression that Wilson is waging a personal vendetta against Smith. Whilst I would personally welcome the presence of a Brit force in Zambia the situation is explosive. Kaunda is being subjected to violent Communist pressure from the OAU [Organisation for African Unity] countries that want an all-out war against Rhodesia backed by British forces! I trust this will never happen. Smith quite rightly has said that he has every intention of sticking to his side of the bargain regarding Kariba and will not interfere with the power. He cannot stop sabotage on the Zambia side. Rhodesia could handle any force from purely African states, but not if supported by any Western Power. Just look at what 350 white mercenaries could do in the Congo against 35,000 guerrillas. There are the seeds of a first-class show down unless Wilson & Bottomley are prepared to be less communistic in their views & talk less. You have no idea what is going on in places like Ghana, Kenya, Uganda, etc. There isn't a vestige of democracy left. Apart from the one party state by the ruler, violence, corruption & inefficiency are rife.

Letter 20 January 1966

It is with mixed feelings that I am writing this letter to you. Frances and I naturally are feeling this present stupid mix-up very much more than the average white Rhodesian, the majority of whom have never seen England and therefore have no loyalty except to Smith & Co. But those who, like ourselves, look upon Rhodesia as the country of their adoption & regard Britain as their home, are certainly feeling very anti Wilson & his blasted Labour Party. Trade sanctions & embargoes are fair enough but when it comes down to interfering with pensions, imposing sanctions on telecommunications & posts it all becomes rather pathetic. We gather that from next week no letters from Rhodesia will be accepted by any P.O. in Britain – likewise telegrams. Of course this can be circumvented but it involves a great deal of extra trouble and expense.

... If tobacco this year is a complete & utter flop I may decide not to grow a crop next year & just concentrate on a 200-acre maize crop. Our crop this year will very likely be bought by the Government at a knock-down price. If I can cover costs and make no profit I will be thankful. The really disturbing problem that is facing the farming community is this drought. It is supposed to be the worst in living memory. In the southern half of Rhodesia, known as Matabeleland, cattle are dying at the rate of 700 to 1,000 a day. Crops are virtually

non-existent & the whole area is being dealt with under drastic drought emergency regulations. We up in Mashonaland are not so badly hit though both the tobacco and maize, which in early December looked so promising, are now not likely to produce more than 40% of the anticipated yield. So, all in all, the picture is gloomy & there is nothing whatsoever one can do about it. There is no doubt at all that a good farmer needs to adopt a fatalistic, philosophical attitude towards life. I'm slowly acquiring it.

There has been a spate of visiting MPs here, both Labour & Conservative. I had lunch with Patrick Wall on Tuesday. He & Julian Amery & Sir John Barlow have been visiting SA & Rhodesia on a fact-finding mission. Very wisely they didn't go in for public meetings as three young Labourites did – Messrs Rowland, Ennals & Bray. These misguided politicians tried to hold a public meeting in Salisbury last week & got shoved around. It was a bad show & all sane-thinking Rhodesians utterly disapprove of this whole thing. But unfortunately, amidst & amongst the Rhodesian Front's most avid supporters are the Afrikaans element & many artisans from Britain. Patrick Wall was most adamant that Britain would have to open negotiations with Smith. Not only was the Rhodesian economy being completely ruined & never likely to pick up again, but Britain too was suffering a very substantial financial setback.

Though Wilson has said all along that he discounts the use of force over here, we now hear that possibly force may have to be used as a last resort when, in his (Wilson's) opinion, the time has arrived when as the result of economic sanctions Rhodesia is on her knees & the forces of law & order require bolstering up by British troops!!! Believe me when I say that never has a man been so misguided as Wilson. Sanctions, though

crippling, will never by themselves make Smith capitu-
late. These Rhodesian Fronters are fanatical & have
very much the same sort of fervour as the Boers had in
1898–1900. They won't submit & will not negotiate un-
less the more sensible & intelligent people in their ranks
can oust the real fanatical racialists & Negro-phobes.
There are many people of serious good will in the coun-
try who are imploring Smith to come to terms. After all,
who would willingly & with complete & utter abandon
rush into complete & utter financial ruin? That is what
Rhodesia is doing here. Possibly Sir Hugh Beadle the
Chief Justice who is at present in London speaking to
the British Government may return with some worth-
while offers. I sincerely hope so.

What do you think about Nigeria [suffered a coup in
January 1966] – the one African state that was always
being held up as a model of democracy & efficiency?
Rather shattering, really, although those people who
lived there forecast that this would happen. After all,
it all boils down to tribalism & with so many factions
and over 200 dialects what hope for a Federation to
succeed. Poor old Abubakar Tafawa Balewa. I expect
they'll find his corpse stuck down some ant hole. When
you really get down & compare what is going on in all
African independent states where there is so-called ma-
jority rule, though the elections are universally rigged,
& see how poor old Rhodesia is being run, there just is
no comparison.

Letter 18 April 1966

V many thanks for your long & newsy letter with your
warm Easter wishes. Well might you be worried about
us. We too are far from being complacent & with each
new development in the whole Rhodesian situation

we feel increasingly despondent. Smith is not going to budge an inch & nor is Wilson. The latter's action in using force to divert oil tankers is being considered here as scandalously deceitful, especially as he promised that force would not be used. Tempers & feelings are running extremely strong. Frances & I, realising the delicate implications & never having been 'Smithites', as well as bitterly opposing UDI, do sometimes think that British politics verges on the perfidious. 'Perfidious Albion', as Napoleon dubbed us, is not always untrue. Unless Wilson & Smith are prepared to get round a table & talk, this whole absurd situation could very easily blow up into a first-class show-down involving SA & Portugal.

You might well wonder what the result of the tobacco sales will be. They are being held in the most closely guarded secrecy & no grower knows what is happening. My first sale averaged 2 1/2 pence per pound!!! Last year I would have received 24 to 30 pence per pound. If I average a shilling a pound for the whole crop I'll be lucky & will be down some £2,500 on costs. Thousands of growers will not be in a position to put in a crop this coming season. I certainly won't & will endeavour to concentrate on maize, ground nuts & beans. Credit facilities have dried up & loans & overdrafts are almost impossible to get. It might sound terrible to you but even I, who am usually v prudent, always have an overdraft of up to £6,000 at this time of year; that is when the tobacco crop is about to be sold. The economics of farming are alarming; a drought like this year can put you in the red, or too much rain can do likewise. Add economic sanctions & the whole picture is just about as clear as pea soup. Doubtless we'll pull through.

I hope no subversive African decides to fire my 200-acre maize crop which, in a few months' time, will be as dry as tinder & ready to reap. Crop destruction, maim-

ing of stock & arson are favourite practices amongst the political agitators. We certainly never have a dull minute. But we pray earnestly that sense & goodwill will prevail. One must concede that majority rule will come here within the next ten years. That is what the moderates think. No one in their senses can accept it sooner. The extreme right wingers, of course, want to adopt the SA pattern of government.

During this period Dick, along with many of the farmers throughout the country, continued to help with local security with the Police Reserve. Farmers formed mobile patrols in support of the Police (normally four men per patrol), using their own farm trucks, armed with shotguns or hunting rifles, and equipped with police radios. Dick usually ran one of the radio shifts in Norton Police Station for between eight and twelve hours a night as and when required. My father also started going to bed with his shotgun and Mauser P38 pistol (taken from a German during the war) by his side. Some five years later the terrorist war had started along Rhodesia's borders in earnest but did not reach the area around Norton until after my father had died and my mother had moved to Salisbury.

Dick particularly enjoyed the visits of old friends, such as this one by Colonel Irwin, also an 8th Gurkha, who travelled from England to stay at Swallowfield.

Dick's last visit to England

My parents came to England for my wedding to Mary in September 1970.

Getting to know Mary!

Anne and Bill Willett, Mary and Ian, Frances and Dick

Mary's father had won a DSC captaining a destroyer at Dieppe when aged only twenty-three. Her mother was a Canadian who had served as a Wren in the Royal Canadian Navy during the war.

Jerry, Dick and Nigel at Malmaison (Jerry's home) in September 1970.

The last two letters that Dick wrote
to me a year after his visit to England

Swallowfield, 15 August 1971

My dearest Ian,

I fear it's been rather a long time since I last wrote to you and Mary. I expect you will soon be on the point of getting ready to move to Germany. Things in Ulster seem to be getting out of hand. That sort of work is just about the most frustrating and lousiest any troops have to face. I wonder whether the Army will be able to clamp down on the IRA. There are all the ingredients there for a bloody civil war. The Irish question has been a simmering storm for several centuries, one that no Brit Govt has succeeded in solving.

Have practically finished reaping the maize. With luck may get six thousand bags, which is about eight hundred down on estimate. Rather disappointing when all is said and done. At three dollars a bag it is a tremendous battle to make a profit, especially as production costs have increased so drastically in the past few years whilst our end product price is pegged by Govt. There has been no increase in agricultural prices paid to producers since UDI whereas business and industry have whacked up huge increases on everything they make. Naturally very few folk in Salisbury and Bulawayo want an end to sanctions. They are sitting pretty. Hopes of a settlement are fading unless the Rhodesian Front are prepared to concede a few points.

Am having to type this letter because my right arm, which has been hurting like hell for four months, precludes my being able to hold a pen. I have been told by my doctor that the nerves in my neck are the cause. Anyway I've been going to Salisbury three times a week for treatment by a chiropractor, so far without much success. It's all most frustrating because apart from the intense pain I am unable to do the hundred and one tasks which crop up continually on the farm. Ah well, we all grow old and must expect some sort of aches and pains. Mum too has had a very nasty poisoned leg, which is only just beginning to get better. In fact it's all been rather an unfortunate year health wise. This has caused us to make an appraisal of the future as far as farming is concerned. It's all very, very difficult. Am putting in a big crop this year and hope that all goes well. With 24,000 dollars invested in maize and soya beans as well as stock it makes one a trifle apprehensive as to what could happen should I ever go sick.

Life in Norton carries on very much as usual. We don't mix much and never go to the club. In the winter cricket, Norton did not achieve much. Hartley beat the Umvukwes in the final. There is the Salisbury Show next week and everyone seems to be busy preparing for it. Hopelands has a stand and Mum will do her stint. You will be sad to hear that Peggy Grobelaar died last week. She and Leon were a wonderful couple who've both helped Hopelands tremendously. The weather is absolutely superb. Continuous sunshine all and every day. Still very cold in the early morning and at night. I start off the day wearing three jerseys which I peel off one by one as the sun ascends in the sky. Today we have just finished lunch sitting out under the trees in the garden, busily engrossed watching the birds through the binoculars with the two dogs lolling about on the grass. I have to admit that I enjoy being thoroughly idle. If only one had not to earn one's bread and butter. It's nice to know that your academic sweat is behind you and you can look forward to a spot of practical soldiering. How is the German coming along?

God bless you. Much love, Dad

Swallowfield, 29 August 71

My dearest Ian,

It was grand getting your newsy letter of 25th that only took three days to reach us. This brings our warmest love & good wishes to you and Mary on your 1st wedding anniversary next Saturday. What a lot has happened since that happy & memorable day when you & Mary were married. A happy marriage with lots of real true love is a great thing. Mum is trying hard to get me away for a few days to Inyanga in Sept. Leaving the farm is a bind but I will make an effort to get away for three or four days – a few days' break is a great tonic. The old arm still pains a lot, but there is much more movement & I can at last hold a pen. It's a sort of continuous dragging pain in the nerve sheath from the shoulder down to the fingers. One has to learn to live with it I suppose. Well we have finished reaping the maize – 6,000 bags which is 25 to the acre. I had expected 30, but have to be content seeing that the country average is only 17. Profit wise, there is nothing in it at all. I see in today's papers that over 6,500 of the country's 8,000 farmers earn less than $4,000 pa – & between them owe $28M to the banks. The Govt is extremely worried. The only solution is to increase the price we get for our produce. Forgive shaky writing. God bless you & Mary – you are much in our thoughts & prayers, especially just now.

Much love, Dad

Three days after writing this, Dick died from a heart attack. With hindsight, it is clear that the pain in his right arm was a symptom of the undoubted stress he was experiencing. This stress, together with his concern that there was no longer a sustainable future in Rhodesia for a white farmer, may well have caused his sudden and totally unexpected death. He had kept himself fit all his life and was the same weight in his fifties as he had been when he left Sandhurst. He never over-indulged himself and I well remember him often declining a second cup of tea in the afternoons with the words 'No, thank you; one's plenty – two's a sign of weakness!' Other favourite quips of his, always delivered with a twinkle in his eyes, were: 'You should always leave the table being able to eat the same meal all over again. If you can't, you've eaten too much!' 'Look at that person [in a restaurant, tucking into a huge helping] digging his or her grave with their teeth!' 'If God had wanted us to spend our entire time sitting down, we would have been born with bigger backsides and no legs!'

His funeral service was in Salisbury Cathedral. His close friends, including Richard Fleming, carried his coffin, draped with the Union Jack into the cathedral. Amongst the packed congregation from many parts of Rhodesia were most of his farm workers, who had made their own way (some thirty miles) from the farm.

From the Parish Magazine of St Edmund's Church, Hartley:

It was a tragic day for Rhodesia in general, and for this Parish in particular, when Dick McGill passed on. Tragic, because Dick was an outstanding man. A military man, coming from a military family, he served with great distinction in the 8th Gurkha Rifles. A year or two after World War II he came to Rhodesia and settled on a farm at Norton where he soon became a leading member of the Parish. He will long be remembered for his service to his fellows; especially for his creative work, together with his wife, Frances, in founding Hopelands Trust and guiding it successfully for many years. With characteristic thoroughness, he visited and studied similar institutions in other countries so that their informed experience could be brought to bear on the needs of Rhodesia. Nor was he content to organise facilities for retarded children through school, though this in itself represented a very full task; he was determined to secure a future for them in their years after school. He knew, on a personal basis, all the young people of the Hopelands' communities and – what is more – their individual circumstances. Small wonder that they loved him.

From Hopelands

What finer tribute can we pay him except quote from a letter received: *'He was about the only man they know of whom everything was good.'*

My mother could not manage the farm on her own and so a neighbour, Angus Kirkman, kindly offered to cultivate and manage the crop that Dick had so recently planted, ensuring that she received a fair share once it was harvested and sold the following year. Angus also completed the sale of all the livestock and the auction of all the farm machinery after I returned to my unit in Germany once my compassionate leave expired. The farm (both Swallowfield and Thornbury sections) was sold after my mother moved to Salisbury (Harare). She then moved to England with Richard so that she could see more of Julia (by now married and living in Topsham, Devon) and me, plus our respective families. Richard settled into sheltered accommodation in Aldershot and found work for the first time in his life as a kitchen hand in the military hospital. Although my father foresaw inevitable changes in Rhodesia, at least he was spared the turmoil that has overtaken Zimbabwe.

Twenty-one years after my father's death, Mary and I returned to what is now Zimbabwe. We spent a morning at Swallowfield to find the farm in terminal decline. The African owner had pulled down most of the farm buildings to sell the bricks and roofing, but had not cleared up the remaining rubble; he had cut down most of the trees my father planted to sell or burn the wood, but had not planted new ones; the farmhouse was looking very shabby and the garden was dying; there were no crops planted save for a few acres of scruffy mealies spread in a random manner close to the house. Thornbury, however, had been bought by a white farmer, who at that time was serving as a minister in Mugabe's government. He had developed a most beautiful home and garden and had also sunk three boreholes in order to provide a guaranteed water supply for his maize fields.

The two farms reflected, in miniature, the fortunes of much of Africa since the Second World War. We also went to look for Dick's memorial and ashes in the Warren Hills Cemetery, close to Harare but without success until the cemetery's manager, a very friendly African, asked if he could help us. When I told him we could find no sign of my father's memorial on a wall where it had been mounted soon after his cremation, he explained, 'Ah yes, I know exactly what you are looking for and have it in my office behind my desk' and kindly showed us to his office where he gave me the box containing the ashes and the inscribed stone with Dick's details. When we asked why it was no longer on the wall he explained, 'It fell off about three years ago and I haven't got a screw to put it back securely.' I decided immediately to bring back Dick's ashes to England. They were buried next to my mother's ashes in St Bartholomew's Churchyard, Holton Village, near Oxford, in a small family ceremony on a beautiful, cold winter's day in December 1992.

St Bartholomew's Church, Holton.

POSTSCRIPT

A simplified family tree, opposite, illustrates a remarkable 'McGill' record of military service, most of it in India, over six generations and spanning almost two hundred years. Malcolm, Dick, Jerry and Nigel served a total of ninety-five years commissioned service between them.

The brothers' lives were full of challenge but, typical of the humility of so many others from the same generation, they saw nothing remarkable about their experiences. Two constant threads running through my father's life were change and hope. He never saw Jersey again after his last visit home on leave before the war, but always regarded his childhood with great nostalgia and was eternally grateful to his parents, his brothers and his school for giving him the experiences early in his life that later stood him in such good stead. However difficult the challenges he faced later in his life, he had an instinctive optimism. He firmly believed that one 'reaped what one sowed' and he dealt with people exactly as he expected to be treated himself. Having been a soldier during the Quetta Earthquake, the Second World War and the Indian Partition and seen how easy it was for people to lose their lives and homes, he never set much store in material possessions but placed far more emphasis on education, training and human values, especially integrity, trust, courage and humour. He went the extra mile to ensure that Richard, Julia and I were given every opportunity to grow, as he also did for the young handicapped people in Hopelands, his farm workers on Swallowfield and everyone for whom he felt responsible. He loved cricket and the maxim 'It's not how long you're at the crease but how many runs you make' well describes his attitude of getting on and finishing whatever he was doing. Like his three brothers, he certainly made plenty of runs throughout his life.

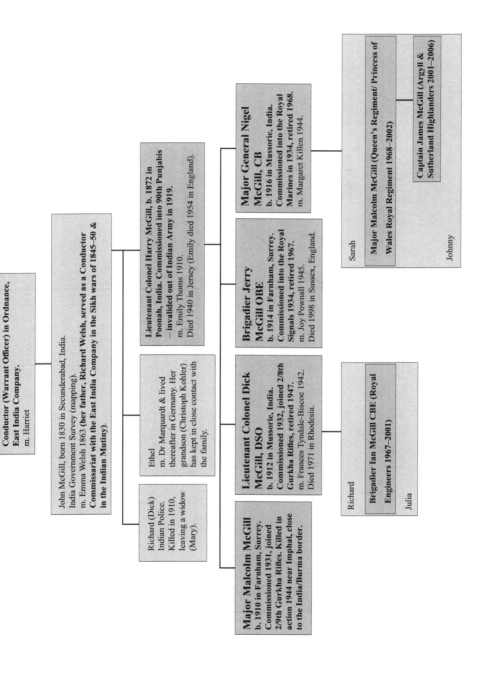

John McGill,
Conductor (Warrant Officer) in Ordnance,
East India Company.
m. Harriet

John McGill, born 1830 in Secunderabad, India.
India Government Survey (mapping).
m. Emma Welsh 1863 (her father, Richard Welsh, served as a Conductor
Commissariat with the East India Company in the Sikh wars of 1845–50 &
in the Indian Mutiny).

Richard (Dick)
Indian Police.
Killed in 1910,
leaving a widow
(Mary).

Ethel
m. Dr Marquardt & lived
thereafter in Germany. Her
grandson (Christoph Kohler)
has kept in close contact with
the family.

Lieutenant Colonel Harry McGill, b. 1872 in
Poonah, India. Commissioned into 90th Punjabis
– invalided out of Indian Army in 1919.
m. Emily Thoms 1910.
Died 1940 in Jersey (Emily died 1954 in England).

Major Malcolm McGill
b. 1910 in Farnham, Surrey.
Commissioned 1931, joined
2/9th Gurkha Rifles. Killed in
action 1944 near Imphal, close
to the India/Burma border.

Lieutenant Colonel Dick
McGill, DSO
b. 1912 in Mussorie, India.
Commissioned 1932, joined 2/8th
Gurkha Rifles, retired 1947.
m. Frances Tyndale-Biscoe 1942.
Died 1971 in Rhodesia.

Brigadier Jerry
McGill OBE
b. 1914 in Farnham, Surrey.
Commissioned into the Royal
Signals 1934, retired 1967.
m. Joy Pownall 1945.
Died 1998 in Sussex, England.

Major General Nigel
McGill, CB
b. 1916 in Mussorie, India.
Commissioned into the Royal
Marines in 1934, retired 1968.
m. Margaret Killen 1944.

Richard

Brigadier Ian McGill CBE (Royal
Engineers 1967–2001)

Julia

Sarah

Major Malcolm McGill (Queen's Regiment/ Princess of
Wales Royal Regiment 1968–2002)

Johnny

Captain James McGill (Argyll &
Sutherland Highlanders 2001–2006)